The growing entitlement mentality in this country is completely toxic, slowly eating away at our spirits like acid. I've said for years that if you want to win, you've got to take responsibility. You've got to leave the cave, kill something, and *then* you can drag it home! Personal responsibility may be the hard way, but it's the only way.

DAVE RAMSEY, *New York Times* bestselling author
and nationally syndicated radio show host

The Entitlement Cure is a powerful book that gives people a true roadmap to success. If you want a better life, starting right now, buy this book.

DANIEL G. AMEN, MD, founder, Amen Clinics,
author of *Change Your Brain, Change Your Life*

Dr. John Townsend has written a helpful and encouraging book to help us deal with the issue of entitlement, whether we see it in others or in ourselves. Overcoming this mindset isn't easy. It requires discipline, honesty, and responsibility. That's the hard way, but it's the only way worth taking.

JIM DALY, President—Focus on the Family

There are so many real-life examples based on John's experience and expertise that reinforce why the hard way is the best way and God's intended way for our success. This is more than a book to read, it's an engaging conversation with a "friendly" expert.

GARY DAICHENDT, former executive
vice president, Cisco Systems

Buying and reading *The Entitlement Cure* should be one of the easiest decisions you ever make. Why? Because we all need John Townsend's life-giving message. Don't miss out on this compelling and immensely practical book. You will love *The Entitlement Cure*!

DRS. LES AND LESLIE PARROTT, authors of
Saving Your Marriage Before It Starts

There are no shortcuts to anywhere worth getting to. *The Entitlement Cure* is full of wisdom, truth, empowerment, and principles that will help you and those around you actually achieve success. I've been waiting for this book and could not put it down. It is a new word for our generation.

CHRISTINE CAINE, founder, The A21 Campaign

There is no such thing as "the easy button," but my friend John Townsend delivers real remedies to today's entitlement mentality. *The Entitlement Cure* is a game changer.

DR. KEVIN LEMAN, *New York Times* bestselling author
of *The Birth Order Book* and *The Way of the Shepherd*

Dr. John Townsend is one of the leading psychologists in the world today, and his new book, *The Entitlement Cure*, will help hundreds of thousands of readers. He describes the hard way as developing the habit of doing what is best, rather than what is most comfortable, to accomplish worthwhile outcomes. In reality, the hard way actually becomes the easiest way to achieve success and love. I highly endorse this book.

PAUL MEIER, MD, founder of the
national chain of Meier Clinics

The only place where "success" comes before "work" is in the dictionary. Cutting corners is a shortcut to losing—there is no free lunch. John has hit on one of the most pressing problems facing families, businesses, and society. We have a rising culture of entitlement. *The Entitlement Cure* is a straightforward illustration and guide to curing this epidemic.

C. KEMMONS WILSON JR.,
founding family of Holiday Inns

Dr. John Townsend has addressed a devastating result of the disappearance of personal responsibility in our culture—*entitlement*. He provides the necessary tools to identify it and a system to deal with it. *The Entitlement Cure* is a useful addition to everyone's toolbox.

BILL YINGLING, former chairman and CEO,
Thrifty Corp

John has again demonstrated a clear understanding of the reality we all face of feeling entitled about something. With his explanation of the hard way in his new book, *The Entitlement Cure*, we learn of a path forward, always learning to be vulnerable, affirming others appropriately, taking risks, and knowing the "why" whenever we do something.

GREG CAMPBELL, former executive VP/Partner
Coldwell Banker Corporation

THE
ENTITLEMENT
CURE

Also by Dr. John Townsend

Boundaries with Teens

Beyond Boundaries

Hiding from Love

By Dr. Henry Cloud and Dr. John Townsend

Boundaries

Our Mothers, Ourselves

Boundaries in Marriage

Safe People

Boundaries in Dating

How People Grow

NIV Life Journey Bible

*12 Christian Beliefs
That Can Drive You Crazy*

Raising Great Kids

Making Small Groups Work

How to Have That Difficult Conversation

THE ENTITLEMENT CURE

FINDING SUCCESS AT WORK AND IN RELATIONSHIPS IN A SHORTCUT WORLD

DR. JOHN TOWNSEND

ZONDERVAN

The Entitlement Cure
Copyright © 2015 by John Townsend

Requests for information should be addressed to:
Zondervan, 3900 *Sparks Dr. SE, Grand Rapids, Michigan* 49546

ISBN 978-0-310-35339-3 (softcover)

ISBN 978-0-310-41297-7 (audio)

ISBN 978-0-310-41296-0 (ebook)

Library of Congress Cataloging-in-Publication Data

Townsend, John Sims, 1952–
    The Entitlement Cure : finding success in doing hard things the right way / Dr. John
  Townsend. — 1 [edition].
        pages   cm
        ISBN 978-0-310-33052-3 (hardcover)
        1. Success — Religious aspects — Christianity. I. Title.
  BV4598.3.T69   2015
  170'.44 — dc23   2015015677

Published in association with Yates & Yates, www.yates2.com.

Cover design: James Hall
Interior design: Kait Lamphere

First printing August 2018 / Printed in the United States of America

To all who live life the hard way,
because life works best that way.

CONTENTS

ACKNOWLEDGMENTS

Elaine Morris, for the many, many accountability phone calls to help me stay on track in the writing process;

Sealy Yates, my literary agent, for your continual excellence in cocrafting my writing career, and a great friendship;

Sandy Vander Zicht, executive editor at HarperCollins Christian Publishing, for encouraging me to write from passion and interest in this topic;

Mark Schoenwald, president and CEO of HarperCollins Christian Publishing, for your leadership and for your support of this project;

Steve Halliday, my writing coach, for your insights into making this book an integrated whole;

My wife, Barbi, for your love, presence, and suggestions during the writing process;

My men's group, along with Greg Campbell and Scott Makin, for your steady support in creating this book;

The Townsend Leadership Program team members, for letting me try out the concepts and skills in the material;

The Townsend Institute of Leadership and Counseling, for using this book content to train others in their fields of competence;

Christine Ames and Deana Vollaro, my assistants, for creating and following through with a writing schedule that worked.

And to several people who provided their thoughts and personal experience narratives: Dave Bradley, Dennis Del Valle, Dan Granger, Richard Halderman, John Hersker, Paul Rasa, Benny Townsend, Ricky Townsend, Bob Whiton, Brian Williams, and Wayne Williams. Your insights and vulnerability made this a better book.

CHAPTER 1

THIS DISEASE HAS A CURE

Two stories, two different worlds, same problem.

A couple contacted me about some trouble with their twenty-five-year-old son, who was still living at home. He had quit college and was unemployed after losing several minimum-wage jobs. He spent his days playing video games with his friends and his evenings partying. The couple had tried everything to get their son motivated to move on in his life. They'd had friends give him job interviews and had tried to get him interested in an online degree, at their expense. After more than a year of no changes, they were at their wits' end.

We met in my office in southern California. Dad had driven from his office and wore an open-necked dress shirt, slacks, and a frustrated expression. The son, in jeans and a T-shirt, sat with arms crossed. His facial expression and his overall manner were detached, as if expressing that nothing anyone said here would matter. Mom sat between them, in jeans and a blouse, anxiously looking back and forth between her two men.

As the discussion progressed, it quickly became clear that parents and son did not see life the same way. In fact, their viewpoints could not have been more polarized.

Mom and Dad had grown up in a middle-class environment and had worked their way through college. Both had continued to work through the child-rearing years. They believed that taking responsibility made you a better person.

Their son, on the other hand, had grown up in better financial circumstances than either of his parents had enjoyed as children. Yet, though he'd been given more, he gave less. He had no interest in work and a great deal of interest in having fun.

When I asked him about his side of the situation, he spoke at first about wanting to get on with his life. He had a plan to leave home and begin a career, he said, but his parents just weren't patient and encouraging enough. He blamed them for his lack of progress. "If they would get off my back and support me," he said, "I'd get my life together faster."

I kept digging away with questions, probing to expose how he *really* felt. Finally, we got to the core of things: "Why should I leave?" he said. And when I asked what he meant, he replied, "Things are fine. I have a nice home and I have fun with my friends. The only problem is their attitude. If they would chill out, it would all be great. *I'm their son. They owe me.*"

I sat back, looked at each of them in turn, and said, "He's right about one thing: As far as he's concerned, things are fine. He has a comfortable living situation that he likes, and he has to do little to earn it. As long as he thinks you owe him this, nothing is likely to change."

Now shift gears. A different situation, this time a business scenario. I consulted with a company that had an energetic and extroverted sales manager, but whose team was just not pulling in its numbers. Her people had serious performance problems.

I interviewed her in her office. She was in her late thirties, dressed in an understated business-casual style. Pictures of her kids and husband adorned the walls. At the beginning of our session, she was defensive, insisting that her boss hadn't made his expectations clear and that he had not resourced her with enough staff and data to do her job properly. But I had already received information from her boss showing that this wasn't true. The company had done a good job of setting her up for success; she simply hadn't produced.

Finally, I said, "You're a very relational person. I think you are friendly and warm with others, and you work hard. But still, apparently, you aren't closing deals, nor is your team. The company's expectations—"

She interrupted: "Really, though, shouldn't that be enough? I'm a good person, a caring person. I hold this office together with my relational skills. And this company wants me to turn that off and become a work machine with no personality. *I deserve to be appreciated for the things that I do for the company.*"

No matter what I did or said, I could not move her from the position that her relational skills should be enough, even if sales failed to come in. I knew I had a difficult assessment to give her boss.

The Universal Disease

Do you see the common thread in these two incidents? In both cases, the individuals preferred doing life the way they wanted to, and they felt comfortable with their choices. They had little interest in performing difficult behaviors that didn't come naturally to them.

And both of their lives had stopped working.

The most important commonality, however, is that both expressed attitudes of *entitlement*. Entitlement is the belief that *I am exempt from responsibility and I am owed special treatment.*

Entitlement is: The man who thinks he is above all the rules. The woman who feels mistreated and needs others to make it up to her.

I need you to understand the concept of entitlement thoroughly, so that you can recognize it and help others get past it. It is not always easy to understand. Entitlement is *not* the person who has needs or struggles that she cannot deal with on her own. She is in need. Chronically ill individuals and disabled veterans often are in great need of help, and we need to help them. Entitlement *is* the person who is capable of taking care of himself and still expects others to do that for him, because he feels he is owed that. This includes the able-bodied adult child who continues to live with his parents, refusing to work, to contribute to the home's upkeep, or even to clean up after himself. It can also include the worker who takes advantage of disability benefits after she has recovered.

Entitlement is *not* the person who keeps trying to please her boss but lacks either the skills or the clear instruction from management to perform well, and who is therefore always getting poor job evaluations. Entitlement *is* the person whose poor job evaluations result from her refusal to invest herself in her job and who consistently underperforms, not because she lacks the skills or hasn't received clear instructions from management but simply because she sees no reason to; she believes she deserves that paycheck for reasons completely unrelated to how well she performs, and that the company is lucky to have her.

Entitlement is *not* the spouse who feels inadequate because her partner is always expressing his frustration with their marriage and with the role she plays in it, even though she tries hard and wants things to be better. Entitlement *is* the spouse who thinks everything going wrong in their marriage is his partner's fault, and that if she doesn't shape up, she just might lose him. Since he has already made all the contribution to their marriage he needs to just on the basis of who he is, he's completely justified in just sitting back now and waiting for his wife to fix whatever's wrong, without any help from him.

There are many more examples, but the many faces of entitlement will always have at least most of these characteristics:

1. An attitude of being special—"I'm exceptional—and in fact, I'm of far greater value to this marriage (or family,

or company) than the rest of them, and that's why I deserve special treatment. They're lucky to have me."

2. An attitude of being owed, of deserving something — "I didn't create this situation — *they're* the ones who are always complaining. So why should I do all the work, or even any of it? As far as I'm concerned, I should just stay in my office till they've cleaned up the mess. And my bonus had better not be any smaller than any of the others because of it."

3. A refusal to accept responsibility — "Why do they want me to pay rent? I didn't ask to be born. Besides, this will still be their house after I move out. And I can't pay rent anyway, because I don't have a job. None of the dead-end jobs around here are worth my time and effort. And there's no reason I should do my own laundry — Mom has to do hers and Dad's anyway — she can just do mine at the same time. It's no extra work."

4. A denial of one's impact on others — "Sometimes my husband and kids' lack of responsibility bothers me, and I say exactly what I feel. I'm telling them the truth. I don't sugarcoat it and I don't tone down my language, my volume, or how long I talk. They overreact to what I'm saying, and that's their problem. It's a free country, and I can say what I need to say."

Whatever the cause of the sense of entitlement, the end result is that the person believes that he or she doesn't have to play by the rules of responsibility, ownership, and commitment. And the end result of entitlement is predictable: The entitled person feels good and lives badly, while those around him feel bad about the situation but have more successful relationships and careers.

It's tempting to make excuses for our loved ones (or ourselves) who evidence an attitude of entitlement, but the only effective response is to take responsibility, not to make excuses. People's life experiences may *influence them* toward entitlement. But they don't *create entitlement.* Many people who have suffered greatly in life, experiencing poverty, child abuse, and chaos, still take responsibility for their lives and choices, blaming no one. And there are individuals who have had it all—love, support, opportunity—who nevertheless see themselves as "owed"—by life, by society, by those around them.

This is important to know if you have an entitled person in your life. You may feel responsible for the part you may have played in influencing that attitude, or you may simply feel compassion for their circumstances. And it's certainly possible that you may have made mistakes in your relationship with them. It's possible that life may have thrown them curves. But those mistakes, those curveballs of life, do not create irresistibly an entitlement attitude; if they did, then all people who experienced those things would approach life with an attitude of entitlement, and they don't. At some point in life, people choose entitlement. They direct *themselves* toward an entitled viewpoint. Why? Ultimately, it's because—at least in their view—it is the Easy Way.

We see the word *entitlement* all over the media—when movie stars misbehave, when marriages go south, or when a young person displays extreme selfishness. You can find scores of examples of this mentality in families, in business, and even in the church. Entitlement has profound negative impacts:

- Companies that must deal with unmotivated employees

- Parents faced with raising self-centered children

- Dating relationships that don't work because of an "I'm special, and I deserve more than you're giving me" attitude

- Young adults who refuse to grow up and so go nowhere

- Leaders who expect special treatment because of their position, not because of their character

- Marriages torn apart by the narcissism of a spouse

- Ministries saddled with prima donna leadership

- Professionals who wander from job to job looking for a place that will see them as the *wunderkind* they consider themselves to be — whether they're productive or not

In short, entitlement has become a serious problem in our society, and it's not getting better. It is impossible to calculate its cost in lack of company productivity, family success, relational love, emotional health, and spiritual vibrancy. Our world suffers greatly from a culture that supports entitlement.

The disease is not limited to any age or socioeconomic demographic. In my organizational consulting and in my psychological counseling, I have worked with seriously entitled people in their eighties and with highly responsible individuals in their teens. The disease cuts a wide swath.

Nor does the word *entitlement,* as I'm using it in this book, have anything to do with politics or government programs. The word has, in some circles, become a shorthand for tax-funded benefits to those who may or may not deserve them. For the duration of this book, forget that use of the word entirely. I'm talking about something entirely different — something that's as likely to affect the critic of government programs as it is the programs' beneficiaries.

The Challenge of Living with an Entitled Person

I consistently encounter among those who have entitled people in their lives, three emotions. All three are difficult and negative:

Alienation. Entitled people aren't easy to be around. Their attitude and their behavior produce consequences none of us wants to experience. People who live around an employee, a coworker, a spouse, or a child who feels "above it all" generally feel disconnected and alienated from the entitled individual. We all find it hard to relate to someone who thinks he or she is superior in some way to the rest of the human race and therefore shouldn't have to play by the rules. One father told me, "I remember being full of myself in my twenties. But I did care about how I impacted my friends and family. My daughter's level of entitlement is something else entirely, and I can't relate to it. There is just nowhere to go in the conversation. She simply doesn't care how she affects us in the family, much less how she is impacting her future."

Anger. What does the Bible teach about the daily responsibilities of life? "For each one should carry their own load" (Galatians 6:5). God expects us to spend time and energy carrying our loads of responsibility for family, finances, and other challenges. That's how a successful life works. So what happens when someone in your life takes little ownership of their own load, leaving you to make up the difference? You feel angry, which makes sense. You feel that everything is "not right," because it truly *isn't* right.

Today as I filled up my car at a service station, down an adjacent street a teenager drove insanely fast for one block. From one stoplight to the next, for about a hundred yards, his tires squealed and his muffler roared. Then he stopped, looked around, and smiled at the startled pedestrians. I felt angry. They felt angry. You'd feel angry.

Helplessness. See if this sounds familiar: You speak to the entitled person in your life time and again about the troubling situation, yet see no change. After a few attempts, a feeling of helplessness sets in. It's as if all your attempts accomplish nothing. People often feel as though their reasoned arguments and warnings, all their loving care, fall on deaf ears.

I encounter this feeling of helplessness a great deal with parents, employers, and spouses. They say they have tried every technique and strategy they know. They are on the verge of ending the relationship and walking away. While sometimes walking away *is* the best thing, most of the time it's the feeling of helplessness that drives the choice to leave, best choice or not. This book will give you more options.

Pocket Entitlement

I'm describing a set of negative attitudes and behaviors that affect us all.

All of us exhibit some level of entitled attitudes, even highly responsible and giving people. It's just part of the human condition. I call this *pocket entitlement*. I have it, and so do you. Later in the book, I'll show how to deal with it. The disease infects all of us, although it affects some more than others.

This book was written primarily to help you help loved ones and associates who struggle with the entitlement disease. But because we *all* struggle with that disease in some way — because we all struggle with pocket entitlement — you'll find that many parts of this book address the issues in a more general way, directed as much to you and to me as to the ones we want to help. In truth, all parts of the book are equally applicable to those of us who want to clean up our own act and those children, spouses, and coworkers we want to guide through dealing with their own entitlement issues.

Enter the Hard Way

There is a solution to entitlement, which I call the *Hard Way*. The Hard Way is the entitlement cure. It is a path of behaviors and attitudes that undo the negative effects of entitlement, whether in ourselves or in others.

Here's my definition of the Hard Way:

> *The habit of doing what is best, rather than what is comfortable, to achieve a worthwhile outcome.*

When you deem something worthwhile, be it a career or financial dream, a great family or marriage or some self-care goal, you have two ways to go about it. Entitlement directs you to give the minimum, find the shortcut, and think only of yourself. The Hard Way takes the opposite tack. This habit focuses on doing whatever is best to reach the good goal, *even if it is difficult, uncomfortable, takes longer, and requires more energy.*

Does that sound hard? Yes, it does, because yes, it is. It's hard to wake up early in the morning and work out. It's hard to get to work on time. It's hard to spend hours a day inputting data when you are a creative person. It's hard to think creatively when you are more linear. It's hard to have difficult conversations, to face down tough challenges, and to do the same actions, over and over again, that are required to achieve success. As the saying goes, it's called work for a reason. But it pays off, just as good sowing leads to good reaping.

Are you hearing biblical echoes in this language? That's because this is a highly scriptural concept: "Enter through the narrow gate. For wide is the gate and broad is the road that leads to destruction, and many enter through it. But small is the gate and narrow the road that leads to life, and only a few find it" (Matthew 7:13–14).

If you have a difficult relationship with an entitled person or group, or even if you have discovered entitlement in yourself, understand this: It doesn't have to stay this way. The Hard Way principles *work*. I have used them in many, many situations and relationships. In fact, the two examples I cited at the beginning of this chapter both worked out well when the entitled individuals applied the principles and skills described in this book. The steps are both practical and effective. If your entitled person has little interest in changing, then you of course can't force them to change—but you will find help here to enable you to deal with the situation.

God originated the Hard Way, and he lives it. All through the Bible, he does the best thing, even if it is a difficult thing. He never avoids it. The best example of this is Jesus, who suffered and died for no other reason than his love for a world that didn't want him: "Because the Sovereign LORD helps me, I will not be disgraced. Therefore have I set my face like flint, and I know I will not be put to shame" (Isaiah 50:7). Setting his face like flint, Jesus faced a way harder than any of the rest of us have ever had to face and created a path for us all to be redeemed and to live.

Ultimately, the Hard Way is simply God's Way. It is how he runs the world, expresses his own values, and makes choices that affect us. You might even call it the righteous path, for it is the right and good way to live: "Thus you will walk in the ways of the good and keep to the paths of the righteous" (Proverbs 2:20). God's ways will never fail you, even when they make you uncomfortable for a while.

The Promise

Any book that recommends "the Hard Way" as an entitlement cure needs a big promise, so here it is: If you learn the principles in this book and live them out, you will experience several positive outcomes:

- *A path to reaching your own goals and dreams.* It's the best way to get where you need to go.

- *Better-quality relationships.* Hard Way people attract good people, and they have a good influence on entitled people.

- *A clarified career and job direction.* The Hard Way provides you with great focus and energy.

- *A way to face and solve challenges.* Whether our own personal attitude toward life is entitled or not, life throws us curves, and these principles will help you to avoid getting derailed.

- *Better self-care and life balance.* You will find here the habits necessary to be healthy and whole.

- *Spiritual growth.* God draws near to those who follow his Hard Way path.

My use of the term *Hard Way* may imply that there's another side to the coin, an Easy Way. But in reality there is no Easy Way, at least in the sense of a life of comfort, devoid of work and struggles. There is only the Hard Way—and the Hardest Way. You do not want the Hardest Way, because it yields the rotten fruit of entitlement. Ultimately, entitlement fails us. We don't develop the character abilities and relationships necessary to become the people God intended us to be. We won't be able to love those who can love us well. We can't succeed in the tasks and missions God has prepared for us.

Choose the Hard Way. It truly is the right way.

CHAPTER 2

THE DEEPER STORY

ONE OF MY CLIENTS is a successful business owner with a history of entitlement. As a young man, he thought he deserved special treatment, considered himself better than others, and in general made himself difficult to be around. He was far more than a disruptive class clown (although he was that, too). He flouted school rules and disrespected and insulted teachers. The parties he organized routinely got out of control. Finally arrested on a serious charge, he was defensive and blamed everyone but himself.

Nowadays, however, he is known as a compassionate yet hard-driving boss, well liked and respected.

"I'm writing a book on curing entitlement in our culture," I told him. "As a guy who has recovered from it, what was the key for you?"

He thought a moment and replied, "Life had to kick me around a lot."

Knowing his past, I agreed. This man had suffered relational losses, financial hard times, and a lack of respect from the public before he finally turned things around. Without question, he had been kicked around.

"I don't think that's all of it," I answered. "I know a lot of people kicked around by life who are still totally self-absorbed and making life hard for themselves and the world."

"True," he said. "A lot of people I know have crashed worse than I have, and they're still not getting it."

"I think the second piece for you," I said, "was that, at some point, *you decided that you had contributed to your misery and that you were the key to removing your misery.* You stopped denying, blaming, and excusing, and looked at the guy in the mirror. That's when everything began to change. It was more than your suffering; it was how you interpreted the cause of your suffering. That's what caused the shift. There's a saying that 'we change when the pain of staying the same is greater than the pain of changing.' You hit that tipping point and decided that the time had come to change. But not everyone does—a lot of people will either remain in their pain, continuing to hit their heads against the wall of reality, or else someone keeps rescuing them from it."

"That's pretty much what happened to me," he admitted. "Eventually my parents and my friends decided not to enable my bad behavior, and when I got sick of the pain, that was my tipping point. I just wish I had done all of this sooner!"

Why We Need to Know How

My friend is a classic example (and I know many) of a person who has turned around his life by jettisoning his entitled attitudes and behaviors. Whether you're suffering from the effects of your own attitude of entitlement or from the entitled behavior and attitudes of others, there is hope! I have learned over the years what works, what helps, and what makes a difference. This book collects the wisdom gained in those years.

But first, I think it's important to understand what *causes* entitlement. If you recognize the process that creates this poisonous mentality, you're halfway there. In medicine, a good diagnosis is half the cure. This chapter explains how people end up with the entitlement disease; the rest of the book explains how to cure yourself and others. Help prevent the spread of the infection!

The best way to impact a family, a business, a church, or a country is through individuals. When individuals see reality, understand what life requires, and get motivated and resourced to grow and change, the entire world changes. Jesus did it with twelve ordinary people. So when you read about the Entitled Culture, remember that the attitude we're discussing in this book infects a great many individuals. Help change the entitlement attitudes in the individuals around you, and you help change the entire culture.

Here's another reason for including this chapter. I wrote it *so that your frustration and irritation with entitled individuals doesn't prompt you to give up on them.* I run into a lot of attitude and personality issues in my work, and of all of those issues, entitlement creates the most impatience in those around the one who evidences it. It isn't fun to be around entitled men and women. Entitled individuals are hard to reach, and they show little concern for their negative impact on others. Entitlement destroys relationships and marriages. It alienates. It costs businesses a lot of money, often through a poor work ethic and lack of focus. It's no wonder we get so irritated, frustrated, and impatient!

I often saw evidence of those angry emotions when I started working on this book. People would hear of my project and say, "When is it coming out? I need it NOW! I am so tired of the self-ishness and slackness. When can I get your book for my company/family/kids/friends?" I have never written a book whose topic generated such an intense reaction.

And that intense reaction came mostly from those who work so hard, push themselves to be so responsible, do things they don't want to do just to make sure the family, or business, or organization, stays on track ... and then watch others coasting. *Someone* has to work harder to make up for that coasting, in effort, love, money, or time. It's natural for this imbalance to cause deep discouragement and resentment.

And it's just as natural to feel deep concern over how someone you love is wasting precious time and energy, destroying relationships, undermining their jobs, and so on. Nearly all of us can list people we care about, people we worry about, whose lives are either being destroyed or who are simply not reaching their potential because of attitudes of entitlement.

My writing coach on this book gave me some great advice that shaped the way I approached the material: "Don't write a finger-wagging book that just gets people even more frustrated and feeling even more helpless. Describe the problem, but give people solutions and hope." The same goes for our reactions to the entitled people around us. It's easy for us to wag our fingers, scold, condemn—but that gets us nowhere. Instead, provide hope. Provide solutions.

The well-deserved irritation you feel at entitlement is not a solution; in fact, it tends to feed your impatience and frustration—it could even spur you to decide impulsively to leave the relationship or fire the employee. And that is not a decision that should be made impulsively or in the heat of anger.

Don't let this attitude get the best of you. Instead, "Do not fret because of those who are evil or be envious of those who do wrong" (Psalm 37:1). The principles in this book will help you feel more empowered, more hopeful, and even more patient.

The Case for Compassion

We could all stand to become more compassionate in our dealings with others, even toward the entitled individuals in our lives. Here are three reasons:

1. It's not all their fault. Entitlement comes not only from a person's choices and attitudes, but also from the relationship environment he grew up in, especially the key connections that affected him deeply. To conclude hastily that a person is "just that way" or "chose to be this spoiled" misses part of the truth. It's important to also recognize the underlying causes of that sense of entitlement.

Does this mean that we excuse the individual's entitled behavior? Not at all. Everyone is responsible for his or her entitlement, completely, 100 percent, no matter the causes. A *reason* is not an *excuse*. We are members of both a sinful and a sinned-against race.

2. We all have attitudes of entitlement, to some extent. Each of us has the disease, with varying degrees of severity. Everyone has some sense of "being owed," or of feeling we are "better than." It's an unfortunate part of being human, and part of Adam and Eve's fall from grace.

I make a distinction between what I call *global* and *pocket entitlement*. Global entitlement permeates all of the individual's attitudes and behavior, no matter what she is doing or saying. If you were to follow a globally entitled person for a week, you would observe it in many of his conversations and engagements with others. It would come out at a coffee time at Starbucks, in an assignment at work, through an incident at church, over an argument at home. This person just can't see beyond her own nose and her own sense of being special. This is hard-case entitlement.

But lots of us struggle with entitled attitudes in *specific contexts* of life—not in every situation, but only in certain ones. That's why I call the second category *pocket entitlement*. It affects only a few areas of life and rarely shows up in the others.

For example: A friend of mine is fun to be around and a great dad. But I visited his company one day and saw a very different person. He was demanding and authoritarian—as if the Inner King had emerged. But when we went back to his house, he became the same old guy.

When I asked him about it, he was surprised. He was completely unaware of his pocket entitlement, perhaps because he had no one observing him in both areas of life.

Sometimes pocket entitlement emerges during stress. Recently, while at an airport on a layover on my way to an important company engagement, it came out in me. I was spinning a lot of plates, with time-critical phone calls and emails to answer. When I heard on the speaker system that my plane was delayed, I clearly remember thinking, *Are you kidding me? I'm a decent person and I work hard. There's an executive team waiting in a board room for me, wanting my input, depending on me. I just do not deserve this right now!* I deserved a break, I thought, given the critical nature of my work and how hard I work at it. *They should get me a seat on another plane right now.*

How entitled is *that*? A stressful situation had turned my pocket entitlement on high.

So before you allow yourself to get too frustrated and irritated at the entitled person in your life, remember first to keep taking the beam out of your own eye (Matthew 7:5). The virus has infected us all, since almost the very beginning.

3. Change happens only in the presence of compassion. No matter how self-involved or demanding a person is, compassion can make a difference — in fact, no lasting change will occur without it. If you're trying to help, you will need to be "for" that person — for their welfare, for their success, and for their growth and transformation. We all need the grace of knowing someone is on our team.

A company called me in to help resolve a major conflict between one of the top salespeople and his sales manager. This salesperson was a high performer and routinely led the team in productivity. Unfortunately, he was also arrogant and a terrible team player. He would neither share information nor help others.

The sales manager was worried about her star's entitlement attitude and its effect on the team. But she had an issue with entitlement herself. In her case, it showed up in her reaction to self-centeredness in others. If you wanted to bring out her anger and frustration, all you had to do was bring up narcissistic attitudes in others.

As a result, while the manager was clear about how she wanted her salesperson's attitudes to change, she was also always on his case and very critical. The escalation of hostilities between them affected the entire company.

When I talked alone to the salesperson, I could see that he did indeed have a chip on his shoulder. The entitlement was real. But when I said to him, "It does seem like she hasn't tried to see how hard you do work and how difficult all this is," he actually teared up a bit.

"I know I can be a jerk," he said. "But if she would just say a few good things every now and then, it would help."

And that's what happened. While the manager continued to insist that he show more team effort, she also made a point of asking about his life and affirming what he did well. Over time, his attitude become healthier, and the department rebounded.

If your approach to helping the entitlement-mentality people in your life is devoid of compassion, people will sense that and react against it. Much of this book is about how to help that globally entitled person in your life—and you will *always* have to begin with compassion if your efforts are to bear fruit. Do you recall anyone telling you that you are judgmental, unaccepting, impatient, harsh, or condemning? Before you attribute those statements to the speaker's unwillingness to hear the truth, honestly check out your heart. See if you are conveying acceptance—which is the companion of compassion: "Accept one another, then, just as Christ accepted you, in order to bring praise to God" (Romans 15:7). Of all people in the world, we who belong to Christ should be the most accepting, since we have experienced the grace that the world so urgently needs.

Relational Patterns That Drive Entitlement

Human relationships, whether personal or professional, heavily influence a person's sense of entitlement. Parents, family members, spouses, friends, coworkers, church associates, and neighbors all play a role. We are the product of the relationships we invest in, as well as of the choices we make.

A large part of any growth system, whether management training, church discipleship, counseling, coaching, or family interactions, must involve what I call *de-entitlement training*. No college course has to teach us how to become more entitled! We know the lessons of entitlement by heart from an early age, and we need little training in it. Instead, we have to *un*learn our natural entitlement.

Growth in the Hard Way means that we learn that the feelings and concerns of others are just as important as our own. We learn, in effect, that as we are loved, so we can love others in turn: "We love because he first loved us" (1 John 4:19). All the care, support, grace, and structure we receive from healthy sources then gets used to make the world a better place as we serve, give, and sacrifice.

Let's consider the major patterns that create entitlement. Most of the time, they involve dysfunctional ways of praising, rewarding, correcting, and establishing consequences for bad behavior.

Praise and Reward Problems

We sometimes reward (through actions) and praise (through words) our spouses, employees, children, and friends in ways that can actually harm them, even though it feels good at the time because it seems so positive. But what *seems* positive is not always what is best. A pizza slice or two is positive — but four can cause problems. These unwise reward/praise approaches, although well intentioned, create bad fruit. Remember—these are patterns, not isolated events. Doing these things every now and then would be all right, but when they become trends, they risk fostering attitudes of entitlement.

1. Praising what takes no effort. Rewards and praise are most effective when they focus on an achievement that took time and energy. Most of the time, when praise is at its most effective, that achievement would involve a person's character or internal makeup. To repeatedly praise a little girl for being pretty puts her in a bind. What she hears is, *What gets me loved is something I can't do much about.* She also hears, *My inside isn't important, just my outside.* We all know people, especially women, who have received that sort of treatment. What happens to many of them as their bodies age over time? They become desperate to look young again, since that is the only thing that has brought them love and acceptance.

How would that little girl feel if instead she heard, "You work really hard and you do a good job at school." Now what receives the praise? Her diligence, which she can do *a lot* about. Although her looks will fade over time, her character will not. Her character will grow and blossom and become even more beautiful her entire life.

2. Praising what is required. *Praise should be reserved for those times when someone stretches himself beyond the norm, puts extra effort or time into a task, or exceeds expectations.* It's not about doing the minimum, the expected. No one gets a party for showing up to work on time: "So you also, when you have done everything you were told to do, should say, 'We are unworthy servants; we have only done our duty'" (Luke 17:10).

A client of mine owned a media business. But before he went into business for himself, he'd had a harsh and uncaring boss. This boss had alienated people and ultimately ruined his company, after the rock stars and the high performers on whom he depended all left because they simply wouldn't put up with his behavior anymore.

So my client, having seen the trouble that went with a lack of praise and reward, overcompensated. He went too far in his attempt to avoid being the kind of boss who had so wounded him. He overpaid his staff. He didn't hold them to high standards in their work. He didn't correct them or change their compensation when they underperformed.

His actions created a happy staff. Who wouldn't like such an arrangement? And he truly was a nice, caring boss. But his employees didn't pull together as a team, nor did they perform well. When I saw all this, I helped him restructure his expectations, alter the company comp package, and change the corporate culture to insist on both high performance *and* high relationships.

Things were rocky for a while. Staff members now considered him unfair—after all, they had known only an entitlement-producing boss. A couple of them left. But most of the staff understood that if the company was to survive, a new culture had to be put in place, one that expected performance. Those who stayed buckled down and started showing good attitudes. Because of these changes, the business started flourishing. Don't get caught in the "praise for the minimum" trap!

3. Praising what is not specific.

"You are amazing!"

"You are just awesome!"

"You're a great human being just because you are you."

Well, thanks for that vague compliment. But where do I go with it? Our culture is awash in these exaggerations that have roughly the same value as an empty calorie. Both yield insignificant benefits. Our brains have buckets where information goes.

Praise should go in the right bucket: the bucket of hard work, of being kind, of being honest, of being vulnerable. But the brain has no appropriate bucket for such nonspecific, excessive statements, and therefore is unable to make constructive use of them.

I once praised in this way, until I realized that I did so only because it was a shortcut. It takes little effort to speak such phrases, and I could say them to my wife or a fence post, it didn't really matter. What requires effort is to take the time to observe and relate to a specific person about a particular praiseworthy behavior or attitude: "The homemade soup you took all day to make is amazing." "You are awesome in how you motivate our staff to make more phone calls every day." These statements go into the buckets that count.

4. Praising what takes an ability and creates an identity. We need affirmation when we try hard and achieve well. We also need to know when we have done well in our class, our staff, or our sport. That is why competition can be healthy. The message is, "You are good at what you do." But when the message crosses the line to, "You are a better person than others because of what you do," or "You deserve special treatment," trouble results.

If you are a parent, the right message is, "Great job on defense in the soccer game! You worked hard with your team and your individual plays were excellent. Now go and help the coach pick up the equipment." Top-tier executives, students, managers, and athletes all have to stand in line. Keep in mind that *while your child may be better in ability, she is no better intrinsically.* In the eyes of God, she is no better than anyone else, as the Lord is no respecter of persons (see Acts 10:34).

5. Praising what is not based on reality. One of the saddest things I see an encouraging person do is to give someone hope even though no basis exists for that hope. Buoyed by an encourager who said, "You can do anything you want to," an individual might spend years and all of his energy in traveling down a path that is simply the wrong path for him and that inevitably leads to disappointment.

Do you enjoy the current crop of talent-based TV shows? I do; I love both the talent and the energy. But a pastor at a church I recently attended pointed out that early in each season, you see a lot of train wrecks when individuals work their hearts out trying to sing, dance, or entertain when clearly they lack the skill or talent. "Why," he asked, "didn't anyone love them enough, early on, to say, 'That's not you; let me help you discover what you're really good at'?"

My parents never told me I could play in the NBA if I wanted to, because they knew that while I liked basketball, I didn't have a lot of talent. I am grateful that my parents helped me put my energies into areas where I had more strengths.

6. A lack of warmth. Ironically, entitlement can occur when a person gets little praise, care, or warmth. That might surprise you, but it makes sense.

We all need to know we are loved and accepted. It's a basic human requirement for health and functioning. But when a person has a number of cold, detached, or self-absorbed relationships, he often creates what is called a *defensive grandiose identity*. That is, to protect himself from the emptiness or harshness of his relational sphere, he will craft a self-perception that is entitled, self-centered, and larger than life. That helps keep the hurt and loneliness at bay.

A business client of mine was seriously alienating himself from his staff and family. He couldn't take criticism well, had to feel (and let people know) that he had all the answers, and presented himself as smarter and better than everyone around him. He had put himself in danger of losing both his company and his family.

He and I began digging into who he was as a person. I didn't find in his background a family that spoiled him or praised him in the wrong way. Instead, I discovered that his home life as a child had included two damaged parents who had little interest in reaching into their bright son's internal world, understanding him, and caring for him. They functioned well in terms of providing structure and values. But because they did not offer him warmth, at his core he felt unlovable and ashamed of himself.

As we dug further, he remembered that when he went away to college, he reinvented himself. He tried out for sports, met girls, and got elected to student government. But his attitude went the wrong way. Instead of becoming grateful and caring, he came across as arrogant and superior.

This story has a happy ending. He had enough self-awareness and had felt enough pain that he was motivated to deal with the early hurts of his cold childhood and then do some productive grieving, letting go, and asking for support to replace what he had lost. Almost immediately, he saw his family and company with new eyes. He cared more for them, listened well, and willingly entered their worlds.

Defensive grandiosity is simply a shell we construct to keep negative feelings at bay. When the entitled person begins the process of growth, the shell begins to dissolve, and healthy feelings and behavior begin to form.

Correction and Consequence Problems

People need not only the right sorts of reward and praise but also the right sorts of corrections and consequences. This is the opposite side of the coin. It takes different forms. Companies have HR departments dedicated to solving performance and culture problems, and those solutions often involve communicating hard truths, offering first help and, if that doesn't work, then warnings, demotions, and sometimes letting someone go. Churches have a discipline structure. Parents have time-outs, withholding toys, and curfews. Each of those approaches, unpleasant as they may be, offers people the chance to grow with the right balance of grace and truth.

But when we avoid setting the right boundaries and following up with the appropriate consequences, we can inadvertently encourage entitlement. People young and old need to know the parameters regarding how they should behave. *Their right to do whatever they want ends at the point where it impacts others.* No one gets a free pass on either their behavior or their words.

We need these boundaries because they remind us that we aren't God. Some lines we don't have permission to cross. Israel did not thrive during its dark days when it had no king, for every person "did that which was right in his own eyes" (Judges 21:25 KJV). Some of these lines are good for us, not only because of the reminder that we are human and not God, but also because they help us take better ownership of and self-control over our own lives. When you know where you stop and the other person starts, you tend to better take care of your own backyard.

I have worked with conflict-avoidant boards of directors, CEOs, pastors, parents, and spouses. They all dread hard talks and setting limits. But when they don't address these issues, they inevitably foster an attitude in others that *I have the right to do whatever I want because there is no reality that conflicts with my belief.* In other words, they develop a culture of entitlement. If you're on the board, if you're the CEO or the pastor or the parent, you need to *be* the reality that conflicts with this belief.

That's the message God gave to Nebuchadnezzar when the king thought himself greater than he was. He ended up going crazy for a long time, eating grass like a cow (Daniel 4:33). You probably don't sentence someone in your charge to eat grass. But you may have to say, "No—and if you continue this behavior, I will have to . . ." And then follow up on the warning. Just remember to be loving and be "for" the person you're trying to help when you set limits, no matter how unloving they behave toward you. If you lose compassion, it's harder for them to learn the lesson. You want them to learn to accept and adapt to reality. You don't want their takeaway to be, "I have a mean boss/parent/spouse." *Loving but firm* is both the right way and the Hard Way.

Meet Needs and Starve Entitlement

It's important to recognize that people have real and valid needs for everything from acceptance to support to advice. A desire for something good is not necessarily an entitled attitude. God created us to have needs, so they must be a good thing and something that should be addressed: "And my God will meet all your needs according to the riches of his glory in Christ Jesus" (Philippians 4:19).

You have to learn the difference between a *need*, which should be met, and an *entitled desire*, which should be starved. Meeting a need leads to life, and feeding an entitlement leads to destruction. It comes down to this: *that which creates love, growth, and ownership* vs. *that which creates superiority or a demand for special treatment.* Praising the real person inside—her character—can never go wrong. Praising her false and grandiose attitudes and behaviors is like throwing your money down a hole. Don't waste your love and support. Place it where it bears good fruit.

Skills

1. **Don't forget compassion:** Have you failed to offer compassion to the entitled individuals in your life and sphere of influence? If so, ask God to help you maintain wise and reasonable limits but at the same time remember that their attitude is not wholly of their own choice.

2. **Look at your own pocket entitlements** and take charge of them. What you notice tends to improve over time.

3. **Review the list of the causes of entitlement.** Do you understand the "how" that affected the entitled persons in your life? Check to see how you might have been influenced as well. The rest of this book will help you cure the disease.

CHAPTER 3

GOD'S FRAMEWORK FOR THE RIGHT WAY OF LIFE

"WHAT DO YOU WANT TO ASK GOD, when you get to heaven?"

A friend asked me that question one night over a dinner at which spiritual issues had peppered our conversation. I thought for a moment and replied, "I think I'd ask, 'Are you sure you've done the right thing by letting me in here?'"

He laughed. Then I asked, "So what's yours?"

"I'd say, 'Why did you allow bad things to happen in the world?'" he said.

I nodded. "And why is that the one for you?"

"Because it bothers me so much," he said. "I don't understand why a loving God would allow kids to get sick and die, and tsunamis to destroy everything, and poverty to be so devastating."

I thought for a while, then said, "Yes, those are very, very sad and incomprehensible things. Absolutely. I often feel the same way. And they *are* things we won't know the *why* about until the other side of the grave. But there's another side to the question that is just as important. On one side is the sheer lack of any apparent justice or logic in the universe—all of those things that you've just mentioned don't make sense. On the other side is our own resistance to our creatureliness."

"Creatureliness?" he said. "As in, we are the creature and he is the creator?"

"Exactly," I answered. "I believe that even if God sat down at dinner with us tonight and explained everything, something inside us would still think, *But—if I were God . . ."*

The Heart of the Matter

That dinner conversation with my friend reflects the heart of the issue of how God has designed the world to work and how we should live our lives. There is a right way to live, and it is the Hard Way. It is work, but it *works*, and it will save you countless detours in life. But *why* is the Hard Way the right way?

Our conversation that night also got to the heart of why we have such trouble with God in this age of the Culture of Entitlement. He has established great and universal principles that enable us to survive, thrive, fall in love, find him, find our own mission, and do all of the things that a successful life requires. And yet a part of us always says, no matter what happens, *But if I were God* . . .

That reaction comes from our inborn sense of entitlement. It is not just a questioning of God; such questioning is healthy, and we have great examples of it in Scripture (the book of Job, or the Psalms, for example). It goes way beyond questioning God to disrespecting who he is and how he ordered life. And when we respond in that way, we reject our God-ordained role in the world he created. Entitlement directs us to judge God for how the world works, for the bad things that happen to us that we don't understand, and for things that didn't happen that we desired. Entitlement says, "My way of looking at life is beyond his," because entitlement creates a deep sense of being special and above it all.

The purpose of this chapter, by contrast, is to highlight the great life principles that direct us how to live successfully and to see how the entitlement culture around us wages war against those principles. I will show you how you can be part of the solution to entitlement.

Here's the truth: *The more you experience and follow God's principles (which lie at the core of reality), the better life becomes for you and those in your life.* These principles originate from the God who never shirks from doing things the right way, no matter how hard they are.

God really does want the best for us! And by living according to the principles he's built into the universe, we can experience his best.

A Rejection of Reality

In its essence, entitlement goes deeper than a person thinking, *It's okay if I want to be lazy because someone else will bear my burdens,* or *I'm so special that the rules don't apply to me.* In fact, entitlement goes so deep that it rejects the very foundations on which God constructed the universe. At its heart, *entitlement is a rejection of reality itself.*

Think about it: This means that entitlement actually makes you "crazy," defined as having a break from reality. It blinds the entitled person to what makes the world work. The entitled person sees a problem at her workplace and thinks, *This can't be my fault,* and misses the reality that her attitude did, indeed, cause a great deal of that problem. Another person sees his struggling marriage and thinks, *When she apologizes, then I will,* instead of seeing that he needs to fix whatever he has broken in the relationship, regardless of what she does.

I have worked with enough cases of severe mental illness to say, with confidence, that you don't want this kind of crazy, or its consequences. It will tear you apart and shred your life and your dreams. God doesn't want that for you! Your healthy friends don't want that for you. And *you* shouldn't want that for you.

Entitlement didn't begin with our contemporary culture. It has been around for a long time. You see it in the very beginning, when Adam and Eve decided that they didn't like the limitations that God had placed on them. They wanted to expand their options so that they could be "like God" (Genesis 3:5). They felt restless with the role God gave them; they wanted *his role*.

Entitlement existed even before the creation of the world. When Satan pondered his own limitations, he said, "I will make myself like the Most High" (Isaiah 14:14). He wanted to be "like God," the same carrot he later dangled before our human parents. Of course, Satan actually wanted more than to be "like God"— he wanted to *be* God, meaning without limitations.

Ever since Eden, we humans want to be like God, with all his privileges and power, and—the very definition of entitlement— *we feel it is our right*. Entitlement infects our brains with the notion, *I have a right to more and better; in fact, I am owed that*.

But when we take a look at human history and even at our own lives, what results do we see arising from an attitude of entitlement?

The answer: It has been disastrous. When a country violates a peace pact with another and goes to war, you'll generally find a sense of entitlement driving it and being used to justify it. When a company breaks faith with its stakeholders, often it's because someone, perhaps a CEO or CFO (remember Enron and Worldcom? Bernard Madoff? Any number of recent banking scandals?), has determined that they are above the rules. And when a spouse enters into an unhealthy liaison with another person, the reasoning will often be, "After how I've been treated in this marriage, I deserve better." Entitlement just doesn't operate in our best interests.

Nevertheless, I am hopeful—and, as with all good things, that hopefulness starts with God. He has not left us alone to struggle with a broken culture, broken lives, broken companies, and broken relationships. He is moving among us with his answers and his power. This is where the principles I list in this chapter come in. These principles underlie everything in the rest of this book. All of the insights and skills we need to escape from the trap of entitlement are here, all of them developed through the Hard Way paradigm.

The Hard Way Principles

Five overarching life principles make possible our successful journey on this planet, in the same way that gravity, electromagnetism, and radiation govern the physical world. The Bible teaches these five principles, and research supports them. The crucial thing to remember is that *these principles cannot be violated or ignored forever, and they can't be ignored without cost.* They are larger than we are, for they come from God. Yes, we can disagree with them, shake our fists at them, deny their existence, and insist that they just aren't fair. But that doesn't change their impact and power.

It's like disagreeing with the force of gravity. You might think, *Gravity is really limiting. It keeps us from flying on our own, so I disagree with it.* And at least temporarily, you can act against it. Jump up from the ground as high as you can, as many times as you can. You will actually catch some air—for a second or two. But you will always come down. You can't defy gravity forever.

It makes no sense to ignore reality or to act as if you can successfully oppose it. If you hit your head against a brick wall long enough because you don't like it standing there, the only thing you'll get for your trouble is a headache. How much better (and less painful!) to figure out how to cooperate with and use these principles and forces in ways that create a great life for yourself! To make them work for you rather than against you.

So learn these principles and use them regularly.

Principle 1: Humility and Dependence — We Are Completely Dependent on God

The Creator designed life in such a way that *he* creates and runs things, while the creatures depend on him: "For in him we live and move and have our being" (Acts 17:28). It's like when someone says, "I am in the army." This statement means so much more — it means, "I am a small part of a very large system, within which I live, work, train, raise a family, and have a social life." This is God's world, not ours (Exodus 19:5). We don't own the real estate.

As in my dinner conversation with my friend, our creatureliness is a *good* thing. It is who we are. We belong to God, not him to us. Creatureliness implies humility and dependence. We acknowledge that this is his universe and that he has invited us into it.

Humility is a much misunderstood attitude and deserves clarification. Humility is not about having a negative view of yourself; it's not about eating worms. Feelings of self-loathing have more to do with having a harsh judge in your head, and they aren't good for you. Humility is simply *accepting the reality of who God is and who you are.* When you see the reality of his power, his love, and his care, you more easily see yourself as who you are: a loved creature, a special creature, an important creature, but a creature nonetheless.

Dependence means you look to him for your sustenance, for every breath you take. You are not independent from his care any more than an astronaut is independent from his air tank, or a child is independent from his parents. You receive good care and guidance from God. That is dependence.

When we forget who we are and who God is, life simply doesn't work, at least in the long run. It works much better when we base our decisions and our actions on a firm grasp of who he is and who we are. He designed us that way. A cell phone does great work as a cell phone, but it makes a terrible giraffe. It wasn't designed to serve as a giraffe. Its best destiny is to be the best cell phone it can be. When you fight this principle of God's world, you fight the concepts of humility and dependence and, inevitably, things don't go well.

In contrast, entitlement tells you to be your own boss and determine your own destiny. Entitlement teaches you to say, "You're not the boss of me!" It implies that you can be and do anything you want, demand of the others around you anything you want, and that it's lame to depend on anyone. After all, it's your life, so you need to follow whatever path you choose. But entitlement ultimately leaves you proud, alone, empty, and functionless.

I was once in the middle of creating a business success program. I was spending a lot of time on it, figuring out how it could help companies better connect with their employees, thereby achieving higher performance. But I had a lot of other irons in the fire as well.

I tend to overcommit to things, and when I do, I have to sort out my priorities. In that sense, I'm a happy workaholic. I work a lot, not because of pain or angst, but because I love what I do. But often I go too far, and that was the case with that success program. So as I was trying to figure out my priorities, I talked to one of my truly spiritual friends. "Have you prayed about it?" he asked.

Immediately I felt like a third-grader who had forgotten to bring his homework to class. I really *hadn't* prayed about it; I had just worked on it. I had totally neglected something so fundamental and so basic. The next week, I prayed about the project, gave it to God, told him I'd go whatever direction he pointed, including dropping the whole thing. I said I would follow him. Within another week, my schedule opened up, people came to me wanting the program, and I had the opportunity to create something that really helped companies.

Don't listen to entitlement when it tempts you to become your own boss—to take complete control of your own life. You *have* a boss, and his name is God. Will you enjoy that all the time? Of course not. Sometimes the boss tells you to do hard things. But you'll be better off and happier and will reach more goals—and more *worthwhile* goals—when you adopt the stance of humility and dependence.

Principle 2: Connectedness—We Are Designed to Live in Connectedness with Each Other

Connectedness, or living in relationship with God and others, is the fuel of life. To be fully known and fully loved is one of the deepest and most fulfilling experiences we can have. We live in a relational world and a relational culture, summarized by Jesus' teaching: "My command is this: Love each other as I have loved you" (John 15:12). Love comes from him, and we are to love not only him but each other.

Relationship is based on need. Throughout our life, we will experience stress, frustrations, and hurts. We will be required to make difficult decisions, and we will make hurtful mistakes. The fuel to survive and recover from those obstacles of life comes from the empathy, acceptance, and understanding we receive from others. We also need connectedness in the arenas related not to survival but to fulfillment: encouragement to be creative, innovative, and productive. The Bible points out how much we need each other: "But pity anyone who falls and has no one to help them up" (Ecclesiastes 4:10). Relationships bring the right nutrients to the soil of our lives, so that life goes well.

In every arena of existence, we see this principle at work:

- Children whose parents tune in to their emotional state have better success later in life.

- Marriages in which emotional intimacy thrives can better weather life's trials.

- People with a support system of friends with whom they feel safe being vulnerable have fewer health problems.

- Churches that feature not only good pulpit teaching but also small groups create healthier disciples.

- Companies that pay attention to relationships, as well as to the bottom line, enjoy improved performance.

Connectedness is both an end and a means. Not only does it sustain life, but relationship, in a sense, *is life itself.* People don't just open up to each other so that they will function better, be healthier, and have better lives. Those are side benefits. The primary motivation is: People open up and make themselves vulnerable in relationships simply because they want to love and be loved. We are, by God's design, drawn to connectedness *because relationships fuel us to meet the demands of reality.*

This is exactly where the entitlement mentality does its greatest damage. It distorts the power and meaning of connectedness so that relationships fail to operate with all the force for which they were designed. This happens in two ways: objectification and an unhealthy self-sufficiency.

Objectification. When one person treats another as a need-meeting object or as a dispenser of some desired commodity, that is objectification. People objectify each other sexually. A good listener may be sought out for her ability, but who remembers to ask how *she's* doing? A doctor at a party often has person after person ask about their ailments, with little consideration of his desire to simply hang out and converse with friends.

The self-absorbed attitude of entitlement makes it difficult to see people as having needs, feelings, and lives of their own. Forget "walk a mile in my shoes"—entitled individuals can only envision the lives of others as an extension of their own. They can't enter fully into the experience of the other individual.

I once worked with a management team in a company that wanted me to get its factory workers producing at a faster rate. Management thought the work was getting done too slowly and that current productivity levels didn't reflect the workers' true capacity. When I asked these executives what they were doing to motivate their employees to work more, I expected them to mention things like bonuses, prizes, team outings, and offers for advanced training. No such luck. "They have a job," they said. That was it. The workers should appreciate their gainful employment.

Their answer dismayed me, so I talked long and hard with these execs about their attitude. If that's how they really felt, I said, I could guarantee that the employees would have a similar attitude, but in reverse: "This company is lucky to have me." It always trickles down.

It took a long time, but finally these leaders started seeing their employees not merely as a means to an end, but as people with lives and dreams—just like the executive team. I had to combat a total lack of empathy, and that battle cost the company a great deal of time and money before the executives finally learned the lesson.

Unhealthy self-sufficiency. Another problem that entitlement creates is the conviction that I don't need others to sustain and support me. I'm not talking about healthy self-sufficiency, such as learning to pay your bills and taking ownership of your choices. I'm referring to the self-sufficiency that *denies that we need the support, encouragement, and feedback of others.* Entitlement sees it as weak or inferior to ask for understanding, acceptance, or a place to vent. To admit need conflicts with the entitled person's self-view that she is above all that and has her act together. Entitlement is anti-need; it will cut you off from the supplies that your life requires to carry on.

If you've ever had lunch with a self-sufficient person, you understand how frustrating and empty the conversation can become. We all need to open up and be vulnerable; that is a basic part of God's life system. But open up to a self-sufficient person and you'll gradually realize that your lunch mate can't relate to people who struggle, or even to those who just need human contact. They can seem friendly and interested, but they have little sense of what it means to be incomplete without human nutrients outside of themselves.

Paul expressed a similar frustration with the Corinthians when they would not be vulnerable with him. In an emotional passage, he pleads:

> We have spoken freely to you, Corinthians, and opened wide our hearts to you. We are not withholding our affection from you, but you are withholding yours from us. As a fair exchange—I speak as to my children—open wide your hearts also. (2 Corinthians 6:11–13)

If connectedness is the fuel of life, then entitlement results in an empty tank for the entitled person. And that causes breakdowns in relationships, love, career, self-care, and spirituality.

Principle 3: Ownership—We Have to Take Responsibility for Our Own Choices

God designed you and me to take responsibility for, or to *own*, our lives and our choices. God created a system in which we have a great deal of freedom in how we choose to live. We freely choose whether we will or will not follow God's ways: "But if serving the LORD seems undesirable to you, then choose for yourselves this day whom you will serve" (Joshua 24:15). God had no interest in making slaves or robots who can't own their choices.

Having this freedom to choose means that we own, or take responsibility for, the consequences of our lives. People who have what business research calls "high ownership capacities" do well in life, love, and work. They make their choices with a mind toward the goal they hope to achieve. They see themselves as succeeding or failing because of their own decisions — what is called in psychology an *internal locus of control*. They believe that their choices, which come from within, matter in their destinies.

We feel happiest when we have high ownership. The entire Boundaries series of books that Henry Cloud and I have written focuses on high ownership: Own your part of your job, your marriage, your dating life, your spiritual life, and your health. If someone is driving you crazy and trying to control you, own that you are allowing things that aren't good for you. If you can't say no to people's needs for your time and energy, own that they aren't the bad guy for asking, and that you need to learn to set a limit and say a kind but firm no.

Entitlement, however, erects a huge obstacle to healthy ownership. It does this in a couple of ways: low ownership and externalization.

Low ownership: Individuals who don't take ownership of their lives sometimes live as if their actions have no consequences. They tend not to see beyond the present; their concern is for what they need and desire *right now*. They're surprised when they lose jobs or relationships. Most of us are aware of the basic principle that "If you sow X, then X is what you will reap," but not the entitled person.

My job as an organizational consultant sometimes involves participating in letting someone go. A company client of mine once called me in to deal with the letting go of a key executive. It became complicated. More than anything else, the company heads wanted to make sure that she not feel surprised at the firing. They wanted to make it crystal clear to her, over a period of time, that they had serious concerns about her performance, that they clearly communicated what it would take to turn things around, and that they would give her resources to help her improve. None of this worked, and after repeated conversations, they told her they would have to let her go.

She reacted with great surprise, telling them that she felt totally blindsided. The company heads were dismayed. After all of their efforts to warn and correct her, she hadn't been able to see it. She had a low ownership of her behavior and a track record of great difficulty judging when she was not performing well in her tasks and relationships. Unfortunately, her low ownership played a significant part in both why she was let go and why she felt caught completely off guard by the decision.

Externalization: People with an attitude of entitlement often project the responsibility of their choices on the outside, not the inside. The fault lies with other people, circumstances, or events. They blame others for every problem. Their entitlement prohibits them from taking the beam out of their eye and asking the all-important question: *How did I contribute to this latest problem?* Instead, they default to answers outside their skin. The result? They tend to be powerless and unhappy. They tend to see life through the eyes of a victim. And their suffering is unproductive—it doesn't get them anywhere.

Blame is a first cousin to entitlement. The more you fight the tendency to blame forces outside yourself and instead own your life choices, the better your life will be.

Principle 4: Accepting the Negative — Your Flaws Can't Be Forgiven and Healed until You Admit Them

Are you aware of the judge in your head? You have one. We all do. And he doesn't shrink from making himself heard. My first emotion when I wrote this sentence was to cringe a bit. I thought, *He was tough on me today.* I don't know of anyone whose first impulse is, *I can't wait to hear what my judge has to say about how I handled my day.* We see him as harsh, negative, and condemning of us.

Your judge is your internal guide, the mental voice that makes value statements on your successes and failures. Most people who read books of this type tend to have a rough judge who hands down condemning verdicts such as:

- There you go again! You always do this.

- You'll never get it right.

- Why couldn't you do that better?

- You're letting everyone down.

- You're such a disappointment.

- You should be ashamed of yourself.

- What a loser!

These are all hurtful and deflating statements, and *we speak them to ourselves.* No one has to judge most of us; we do a fine job on our own. A harsh internal judge slows you down, discourages you from taking risks, and makes you not like who you are.

God never intended this for you. He wants you to experience yourself as he does — as someone special who, though flawed, is "fearfully and wonderfully made" (Psalm 139:14). He wants you to see yourself as someone God loves. When we feel about ourselves as God does, we can accept our sins and failings, and those of others, and then deal with them in positive ways: "Accept one another then, just as Christ accepted you" (Romans 15:7).

God made a way through Christ so that we could live with the negative as it truly is, without denying it or minimizing it. In a relationship with Christ, we feel permission to be who we truly are, warts and all. We don't have to hide, pretend, or put our best face forward. We are known and loved just as we are by the one who matters most. This enables us to love others the same way.

The result of acknowledging and accepting the negative is that *the negative then can be transformed.* When you are okay knowing your failings, you can face them, bring them to God and to the people with whom you feel safe being vulnerable, and heal whatever is driving those feelings. This is the key to great growth. It's a paradox, but the ones who run from the negative will suffer from it, while the ones who accept the negative will find the power to change it.

I was working on one of my leadership teams with an executive who was a successful businessman well regarded by the industry. He found it hard, however, to be authentic with others, especially when he felt frustrated or angry. He thought that if he felt irritated about a sales problem or a performance issue, people would see him as an uncaring tyrant. So he compensated by being Mr. Nice Guy all the time, keeping a smile on his face even when he was seething underneath. His judge stayed in control, telling him, *Don't be who you really are, or it will go badly for you.* This caused all sorts of problems for him: maintaining this cover-up cost him creative energy, people felt he wasn't real, and he had an inability to confront effectively.

I had him open up in our group session about what he was like when he felt angry. He found this hard to do because he worried that the group would judge him as harshly as he judged himself.

But he cooperated: He mentioned someone in his life with whom he felt angry and expressed his anger about that—and he really let himself feel it.

The group responded wonderfully. "I don't think any less of you," said one.

"I've felt that way, too," said another.

"I feel like I know you better now," declared a third.

The experience transformed this man. He felt blown away by the acceptance and grace of the team—just the opposite of what he'd expected. Never in his life had anyone said it was okay to feel angry.

When we met the next month, he reported several dramatic changes. He had more energy. He was kinder to his wife and kids. He confronted others well and fairly. And when he felt angry, he said his piece and got over it quickly. The judge in his head was being redeemed, being taught to accept him as Christ and the team had accepted him.

Entitlement does not prompt you to accept the negatives in your life. It drives you away from admitting your flaws, away from bringing them up with people you trust, and away from learning how to deal with them. Instead, the entitled attitude has three directions, all of which destroy your health:

- *Denial.* The person in denial simply turns her back on reality. She refuses to admit her flaws to herself or anyone else, which eliminates any possibility of deep and satisfying relationships. Who would put up with that for very long? Worse, denial keeps her from growing, changing, and transforming. God doesn't heal what goes unconfessed: "Therefore confess your sins to each other and pray for each other so that you may be healed" (James 5:16).

- *Perfectionism.* The person caught in perfectionism beats himself up for failures, minor or major. His standard for performance is perfection, and he offers himself little grace when he stumbles. He constantly scrutinizes and condemns himself, and never makes it to a point of self-acceptance.

- *Narcissism.* The narcissistic person adopts a grandiose view of himself that hides his flaws, which usually lie buried under deep shame and envy. He is so afraid to see himself as he really is that he reacts in the opposite direction, toward the "I'm special" stance, in which he becomes arrogant and selfish and has difficulty feeling empathy for others.

Think about the pressure, stress, and emptiness that accompany the entitlement solutions of denial, perfectionism, and narcissism! God's way is hard because you have to actually face yourself. But his yoke becomes easier (see Matthew 11:30) because you can then experience his grace, and the grace of others, to bear and relate to your real, authentic self—negative aspects and all. This self can then be loved, forgiven, graced, and helped to become a transformed individual, full of grace, forgiveness, and mercy for others.

Principle 5: Finding Our Role — To Live Long and Contentedly, Find Your Purpose in Life and Fulfill It

Life is complete only when you give back who you are to the world. God made you to pass along the good you have experienced. We don't feel fulfilled or in our right space in life until we find our passions, develop our talents, experience our mission, and engage ourselves in meaningful expression of those things to make the world a better place. We receive love. We become loving. Then we give love to others through our relationships and our talents.

God made it this way from the beginning. Listen to humanity's first mission statement: "Fill the earth, and subdue it" (Genesis 1:28). He designed us to bring order and fruitfulness to the world. Therefore, we are at our best when we work hard, do what we are good at, and bring that good to others—whether it be manufacturing airplane coatings, writing music, or selling real estate. This is the "task" part of life, the "doing" aspect, which expresses itself in a career, a service, or a hobby.

Finding your role means that you are giving back to the world over time in a sustained and steady way, and this attitude actually contributes to your living longer. Research indicates that the number one factor in longevity is not social relationships or happiness, but *conscientiousness,* described as persistence, dependability, and organization.[1]

There are two ways entitlement stands in the way of finding your role and finding fulfillment in it:

- **Entitlement limits the person's goals.** One of the most limiting ideas of entitlement thinking is that the end goal of life is happiness: "I just want to be happy, that's all." Entitlement says that the highest good is to be a happy person—but in fact, that is one of the worst endgame goals we can have. People who have happiness as their goal get locked into the pain/pleasure motivation cycle. They never do what causes them pain, but always do what brings them pleasure. This puts us on the same thinking level as a child, who has difficulty seeing past his or her fear of pain and love of pleasure. There is nothing wrong with happiness. But in a healthy life, happiness comes as a by-product of doing what you love, having purpose, and giving back. You don't give your talents so that you'll be happy; you give them because you care and you want to make a difference. *Then* you feel happy. Happiness is a by-product to enjoy, not a dream to seize.

- **Entitlement limits the individual's growth.** The other negative fruit of entitlement is that *it freezes development.* While God designed us to discover and develop all sorts of great abilities and passions, entitlement influences us to stay right where we are. It keeps us from growing, learning, challenging ourselves, or trying new things. It whispers to us, "That sounds really hard and it doesn't look like it's worth it." When we listen to this voice, something inside us goes to sleep. We might become couch potatoes, video addicts, chronic partiers, or simply get in a rut and routine that becomes boring and deadening.

When you find your God-ordained role, then all the unique abilities and strengths God programmed into you from the beginning begin to function together to fulfill your place in the ultimate great story. And even though happiness isn't your goal, you'll never be happier.

Skills

Ponder a few questions that will help you make good use of God's framework for your life:

1. **Which of the five principles in this chapter has proven to be the greatest challenge for you to live out?** In what area of life does the negative influence of entitlement most express itself against that principle: family, work, marriage, dating, or something else?

2. **Think about a person in your life, family, or work who is entitled.** How did he or she get that way? Family of origin? School experiences? Church relationships? Marriage? A season of great loss or stress? Answering this question will help you not only to help that person, but also to focus on using the rest of the book to help *yourself* grow into the Hard Way of success.

3. **Consider God's own lack of entitlement.** Although he is the only being in the universe who deserves to be entitled, his character overflows with humility and love. Ask him to help you live in reality in the way that he himself does.

CHAPTER 4

HELPING OTHERS WHO ARE STUCK IN ENTITLEMENT

NOW THAT WE'VE ESTABLISHED what the entitlement disease is and how it ruins people's lives (chapter 1), how it might come about and why it's important to combat it (chapter 2), and some principles for healthy attitudes to displace it (chapter 3), it's time to address the reason, I would guess, that you picked up this book.

The Blindness

I once had an executive client who, though extremely talented and competent, alienated his employees with a harsh, parental attitude that made them afraid of him. He could not see how severe his behavior had become; his entitlement had blinded him to its impact.

Because we trusted each other, however, he and I had several difficult conversations about his behavior and attitude. I told him that I feared he would lose his business and perhaps even his family if he refused to change. The first few times we talked, he showed little response.

About a year after our work together ended, however, I ran into him again. "How are you doing?" I asked, looking forward to hearing.

"I was pretty angry at you after our last talk," he replied, "but I agree with you now."

He told me he'd started to work on the issues that had caused me such deep concern. I felt glad to hear it, but it saddened me that his entitlement had cost him so much for so long. I don't wish that on anyone.

The principles in chapter 3 and the skills and strategies in the rest of the book will be equally useful to you in dealing with your own pocket entitlement issues and in helping the entitled individuals in your life who frustrate you and cause you grave concern. You know who they are — you probably had them in mind when you bought this book. A loved one, an employee, a colleague, someone at church, a close neighbor — someone you know well has the entitlement disease and is making your life, and his or her own, difficult and unproductive because of it. You want better for those individuals, and you know that a life of Hard Way success will benefit them, their relationships, their lives, *and* your connection with them.

I doubt, however, that anyone is texting you and pleading, "Help! I've got the entitlement disease, and you have my cure!" A great deal of the problem is blindness to the problem itself.

What causes such blindness? Entitlement creates the illusion that *My life and how I impact others are not problems.* This illusion creates an atmosphere within which the behavior can continue. If the individual were, instead, to think, *My life and how I impact others are indeed problems, and they are my problems,* he'd be much more likely to do the hard work required to change. Keep this in mind: Working with entitled individuals rarely succeeds after one conversation. It takes a series of conversations and events over time — but it *does work.*

In this chapter, I'll present an overview of the elements that give you the best odds of really making a difference in that person's life, of really making an impact on her attitudes. Look at this chapter as a tool kit that gives you what you need to help the individual move from entitlement to Hard Way living.

Remember that there are no guarantees here, and also that no one is a project. God gave people free choice, which we must respect. Don't you want to maintain your own freedom to choose, as well? Look at it this way: *You are influencing these individuals to be whomever God designed them to be in the first place.* Even if they show little interest at first, remember that God created them to be healthy. He set up his world in such a way that the Hard Way leads to the best life possible. Whoever they are, a part of them intensely wants this. Finally, never forget that God is on your side—and if he is for you, then who can be against you? (See Romans 8:31.)

And remember: All of us suffer from the entitlement disease to some extent, and that's why, even though this book is written to help you help the people in your life who have the entitlement disease, I'm also urging each of you to apply these lessons to yourself as well. They will help you live more successfully. You will see yourself in these pages!

The Rehab

The process of helping an entitled individual resembles physical therapy. Not long ago, I damaged the rotator cuff in my right shoulder by working out in the wrong way at the gym. My injury didn't require surgery, but I had to go to Dave, a physical therapist.

Dave resorted to a number of techniques to help me. He had me stretch, use rubber bands, get electrical stimulation, and use cold packs and hot packs. He had me work on other parts of my body that had overcompensated for the weakness in my shoulder. He worked on my rest periods and my nutrition.

In time, I came back to full strength. But during the whole period Dave and I worked together, even though we were on the same wavelength about the process, my rotator cuff hurt. The muscle was damaged and angry and resisted our efforts. It had grown used to the old, protective ways of dealing with the damage that I had resorted to before physical therapy began. In time, however, the process worked.

That is much like how it will be with the person you're trying to help. You are Dave, and your entitled person is my rotator cuff. The elements of therapy you will use as described in this chapter give you a broad-brush stroke of the behaviors and attitudes that will help you to help that person. But don't expect it to go smoothly or even quickly.

Check Out Your "Why"

First, why do you want to go to the trouble of helping this relative, this friend, or these employees? To keep your energy and time focused, you must be clear on why you want to do this. Make sure you have good and healthy motivations. All of us find it easy to be driven by less-than-optimal reasons. People get so frustrated with entitlement, and they feel so helpless to do anything about it, that their irritation can color their motives. If you aren't acting primarily out of love and concern for the one you're trying to help, then your reasons are suspect.

Consider some of the "whys" that you should release. Don't allow any of these to become your top motive:

- *To reduce the stress in your life that this person's bad behavior causes.* While this consideration may be important, it can't be your top motive. Why not? Because it reduces the individual to the role of being a bother to you, a project, something to fix like a leaky faucet, it's not very loving. Besides, good boundaries could do a lot to reduce your stress with the person, without the investment of time and energy required to change them. Saying no to someone who undeservingly asks for a bailout is a no that helps you; it's not a transformative experience that changes them.

- *To vent your anger on them.* Everyone gets angry at the entitlement of others. It *is* really irritating! But if this is a project to "set them straight" or to feel a bit of release because you could finally tell them off and show your irritation, the project will fail. Deal with your anger in other ways (prayer, venting to others, working out). Venting is not an effective motive for working with difficult people.

- *To get them to see how they have affected you.* This motive is about you more than it is about the other person. Sure, it would feel good for the lights to come on and for them to say, "Oh my gosh, I am so sorry for taking advantage of you all these years!" And often, the entitled person will *at some point* have the awareness to see her harmful impact on others. But that awareness should serve her growth, not your satisfaction.

Here is the best and highest "why" for you: *I help because I want them to live well, relate well, and work well.* In other words, you choose to help because you know that entitlement damages a person's life, relationships, and ability to successfully complete important tasks. Even at its least destructive, entitlement prevents the person from reaching his full potential. But at worst, she could suffer devastating failures and even an early death.

The best summary word for this "why" is love. You feel motivated to help simply because you want better for that person; that is what moves you to engage with him or her. This is the deepest motive of God himself, who acts for our betterment: "But God demonstrates his own love for us in this: While we were still sinners, Christ died for us" (Romans 5:8). This kind of motivation will convey the grace and care you really feel toward your entitled individual.

Be Clear on the Desired Outcome

Be sure you know what you want to see happen through the process you're about to enter with this person. As life management author Stephen Covey says, "Begin with the end in mind."[2]

The best possible outcome is that the entitled individual *chooses to accept the demands of reality.* This goal encompasses everything. It means that he no longer sees himself as deserving special treatment, or as above it all, or that she can behave any way she wants to without caring about her impact on others. It means that he shoulders the burdens of life and responsibility, knowing that he is making life better for himself, others, and the world.

Entering the Grief Process

One of the most important attitude outcomes in overcoming entitlement is for the person you're attempting to shepherd out of their entitlement attitudes to enter into the grief process. This is a sign that good things are happening. Grief is the emotion that accompanies loss and letting go of things or people we cannot have. Emotionally speaking, working through entitlement tends to go in phases:

- *Denial*: The person denies anything is wrong with her; it's all everyone else's fault.

- *Protest*: The anger she feels when confronted with reality.

- *Escalation*: The acting out she engages in when the reality won't go away.

- *Grief*: The sign that she is accepting that she is not who she thought she was, and is feeling sad about the losses she must face.

- *Adaptation:* Having let go of what needs to be jettisoned, the person lives with an attitude of love, gratitude, and discipline.

You know someone is reaching this stage when he or she begins to express thoughts like these:

- *I wish I could say or do whatever I like, but that doesn't work anymore.*
- *I can't have anything I want.*
- *I now have to do things that I don't want or like to do.*
- *I have to deal with losses of relationship, money, opportunity, and time in my life.*
- *I have hurt people I love.*
- *I have hurt myself and not been the person I could have been.*
- *I must face my regrets because of my choices.*

Certainly these are "negative" thoughts. They are just as negative as confession and repentance, and like confession and repentance, they point life in the right direction. When you begin to hear comments like these, you know that your person is headed toward a great outcome.

But comments aren't enough. You want to see both attitude and behavioral changes, as both are necessary. To say "I get it—it's been all about me and that's not the right way," is good, it's progress—but if it's not followed by better *choices*, it won't bring complete success. It reminds me of one kind of seed that Jesus mentioned in a famous parable: "The seed falling on rocky ground refers to someone who hears the word and at once receives it with joy. But since they have no root, they last only a short time" (Matthew 13:20–21). Great start, poor follow-up.

For the person to begin changing behaviors, grumbling the whole way and resentful of you, but doing it because they fear you, or because they don't want your threatened consequences, *is* progress. It's better than nothing. But it's not the whole picture. Many are the times my kids cleaned up their rooms, feeling irritated at me the entire time, but never once do I recall them saying, "Thanks for being a dad who is developing my work ethic." (The room, however, *did* get cleaned up.)

Researchers who study personal change now take a neurological view of this process. Someone must have the "aha moment"— when the lights come on, the neurons fire, and the insight comes, as with Paul's Damascus Road experience (see Acts 9:1–6). That "aha moment" is necessary, because external change starts best with internal change.

This is only the beginning, however. In the next phase, our neural pathways need to get trained to do things a different and better way. This is where habits come in—habits of regularly thinking about others, of taking ownership and initiative, of doing the right things even if they are the hard things.

I have seen the process start from both directions. Sometimes it will be a clear conversation in which the entitled person dramatically sees what must change. More often, however, it begins with a grudging change in behavior because of pressure from both relationship and reality. The attitude change comes later. The reason it occurs more often in this way is because the entitlement illusion mentioned earlier gets triggered by the initial "threat," and the entitled person believes that he or she must hold on doggedly and determinedly to the "I'm not wrong/I deserve special treatment/I don't impact people negatively" stance. For when these entitled individuals finally do see reality, they may feel sadness, guilt, remorse, regret, and shame for their actions. They know it would be overwhelmingly painful. So they default to the standby position: "It's better to ignore reality and feel okay than to see reality and feel bad." Your job, as a change agent, is to help these individuals overcome their aversion to dealing with reality.

Evaluate Your Equity

Why should your employee, date, child, relative, or spouse listen to you in the first place? Most likely, you have had some sort of conversation with them, perhaps several. Many people with an entitled individual in their life have a naiveté about it called *defensive hope*. This means hope based on no reality at all. It's simply hope based on desires or wishes.

These people hope because they hope because they hope. Henry Cloud and I write about this phenomenon in our book *Safe People*.[3] This defensive hope falsely leads a person to attempt using logic and reason with the entitled individual, over and over again: "I told him so many times that he needed to get to work on time, and it's like he didn't listen." The reality is not that it was "like" he didn't listen; he really *didn't* listen. You need to do more than repeat yourself, hoping that *this* conversation will cause the *aha*. It won't. Instead, you need to evaluate what equity exists in your relationship that will influence him to pay attention. It generally takes a mixture of the following:

The relationship. If you have been caring, loving, dependable, and helpful toward this person, all of that matters. Logged in his brain cells is the history that the two of you have that shows that you are truly "for" him. Your personal appeal to the person can make a difference — something like, "Do you realize that I am 'for' you, even in this tough time, and I want to help you?" You can draw on this. You have earned it over time.

Kindness. Don't start with the warning, "You had better get your act together." Instead, start with kindness: "I care about you, and I want better for you. To tell the truth, I know I can't make you change, and so I sometimes feel a bit helpless." This often helps the person to be less defensive and to see how she affects your life and feelings.

Understanding. Sometimes the entitled person needs to know that the change agent sees her as a good person and understands that not every bad thing is her fault. It helps to say something like, "I know that your job performance problem is caused by a number of things, and that it isn't your intention for things to be this way."

Need and consequences. To state it bluntly: How much leverage do you have? What does the person need from you that can make a difference to him? On a personal level, it might be your warmth, your love, your positive attitude, your strength, or the structure you provide. On a practical level, it might be that as her supervisor you are in charge of promotions, demotions, and whether she keeps her job. As a parent, it might be that he is financially dependent on you. Does this sound manipulative? Rather, it is honest and direct, and *reinforces the truth that actions have consequences.* Think about it this way: *Most entitled people are also dependent people.* They get away with their attitude because someone is protecting them from its consequences. They would crash and burn a lot sooner if that someone refused to make excuses for them, to give them an infinite number of last chances, and to pay for their mistakes. Your entitled person isn't likely to change until he experiences his own dependency and what happens when you no longer act as his safety net.

Community. She may be able to ignore or rationalize you individually, but she'll find it much more difficult to ignore several sane and healthy people all speaking the same message. Interventions with addicts are based on this truth. It has its foundation in Jesus' teachings:

If your brother or sister sins, go and point out their fault, just between the two of you. If they listen to you, you have won them over. But if they will not listen, take one or two others along, so that "every matter may be established by the testimony of two or three witnesses." If they still refuse to listen, tell it to the church; and if they refuse to listen even to the church, treat them as you would a pagan or a tax collector. (Matthew 18:15–17)

The greater the number of people involved, the more powerful the message.

So think through what resources you can tap. Write them down. Talk about them with others who know the individual you're trying to reach.

Begin with a Vulnerable Conversation

Changing an entitlement attitude almost always begins with a conversation between two individuals. Most of the time, the entitled person's stance has blinded him to the damage he is doing to himself or to others. And letting your frustration drive you immediately to drastic measures, such as ending the relationship, asking someone to move out, or firing someone, aren't effective. Start with the conversation designed to begin the process, *even if you have already had many previous, ineffective conversations.* This time, you are doing it in a different way.

This type of conversation has two elements: *vulnerability* and *stating how you experience the entitlement.* One concerns how you are impacted, and the other describes what you see in them.

Vulnerability. Being vulnerable means getting past your frustration and anger so that you can express your feelings of care for the person, as well as your exposure to pain because of their behavior. Suppose, for instance, your mom's entitlement causes her to dominate conversations and tell you and your spouse how

81

to parent. Her attitude sucks all the oxygen out of the room. You have seen how she turns off lots of other people, too, but no one has talked to her about it. Your vulnerable statement to open the subject might be, "Mom, I want a better relationship with you because I love you. I want to support you and get along well with you. But that's hard when you make the conversation all about you and what you are doing and don't ask how my world is doing. It disconnects me from you, and I find myself avoiding you, which I don't want at all." Do you see how that statement opened with an expression of care, need, and concern? No judgment, condemnation, or "should" message is embedded.

Making it clear how you have experienced the entitled behavior of the individual. What I mean by this is, let them know how you see their behavior. They may have no idea that they are like this, or that others perceive them as being this way. You might say something like, "I don't think you mean to come across like this, Mom, but sometimes it seems as if you think I should never disagree with your opinion, and that you have it all together, and that I need you to coach or parent me. That's hard for me to accept."

Statements like this may hurt their feelings, but even so, you have really done the entitled person a great favor. You have given her reality-based feedback that provides a clear bucket, a *category*, for her. You aren't being vague and general (as in, "I just can't get along with you; you come across weird"). You are being specific and helping her with a blind spot. You have provided something for her to think about, to discuss with others, to check her Bible about, and to research.

For individuals to escape from entitlement, it is first necessary for them to understand that they have the disease. Someone has to say something. Otherwise, how can they change? The people I have worked with who have come out of entitlement thinking have *all* told me — and I mean 100 percent of them — that at some specific point someone said to them, in some form or fashion, "You are behaving as though you are more special than others." The statement may have hurt their feelings or angered them; it may even have rocked their world. But it got said.

We change only when we know the issue. As Nathan said to David in regard to the king's own entitlement sin of adultery: "You are the man!" (2 Samuel 12:7). The prophet's clear statement changed David's life.

Your entitled person's response to this vulnerable conversation will actually give an indication of the severity of his or her entitlement. A person with a mild case may feel remorse and sadness; she may immediately express concern about any damage her attitude may have done. If that's the case, you may have just won a friend whose growth you will enjoy watching in the coming months. (I hope you have this attitude when someone points out your *own* pocket entitlement!)

Unfortunately, those responses are in the minority. In most cases, a conversation like this must be followed by another one — usually initiated by you — that steps the intensity up a notch, as explained in the next section.

Move to a Consequence-Based Conversation

The goal of a consequence-based conversation is to provide the entitled person with a dose of reality. In effect, you are turning up the heat from the previous conversation.

Suppose, for instance, you have an adult child who lives at home and isn't working or going to school or contributing to expenses. You have already had several conversations with him that resulted in no change. It's time to escalate to a consequence-based conversation, which will include these seven elements:

1. *You are "for" him*: "Brandon, I care about you and I want you to succeed."

2. *You are concerned about some negative attitudes and behaviors*: "It's not okay that you are still living at home with no job and no school. I'm concerned that you are not facing reality. You're ignoring your responsibilities in life, and that doesn't work in our home."

3. *You yourself have been part of the problem*: "I haven't been clear and firm with my expectations, and I've waited too long to press the issue. I'm sorry about that."

4. *You are establishing definite criteria for change*: "You have sixty days, and at the end of that time you need to be either signed up for community college full-time plus have a part-time job, or else you need to have full-time job and be contributing to room-and-board costs."

5. *There will be consequences if no change occurs*: "If this doesn't happen, then on day sixty-one I will have your things packed. I will give you a security deposit for an apartment, plus your first month's rent."

6. *You want to hear them out*: "I'd like to hear your thoughts about this." (If he has a valid and objective reason you didn't consider, such as a serious health problem you didn't know about, then you may need to rethink matters. Otherwise, hear him out for about three minutes and then press on.)

7. *Again, you are "for" him*: "I'm sorry this has been a difficult talk, but I care about you and I hope you will make the right choices."

(If you'd like to read more about these steps, check the book Henry Cloud and I wrote: *How to Have That Difficult Conversation You've Been Avoiding.*[4])

Keep this conversation simple. You want to be understandable, clear, and also caring. Don't get hung up on the details—it can all be edited. What matters are the overall principles. Just see that you incorporate the basic elements included here. This approach works equally well with a ten-year-old, an employee, a spouse, a friend, or a relative.

Stick to It

Be ready for anger, escalation, resentment, and tirades. Remember who you're dealing with. Entitlement does not recede quickly! But just as God is engaged in "de-entitling" his people, so you are part of that process, too—as we all should be with each other. Here are some suggestions that will help:

- *Don't take it personally.* Ultimately, he is angry at reality, angry that he can't be a little god. It's not about you.

- *Be kind and not judgmental.* Don't give him a reason to make you the problem. You want his fight to be with reality, and you want him to lose that fight. So be nice.

- *Use your life team.* When you find yourself tempted to be mean, or you feel guilty, or you're ready to write off the entitled person—call your life team. Let them listen to you, support you, and encourage you.

- *Remember that ovens take time.* This is not a microwave process. There's no shortcut, no easy approach—this is the Hard Way. Be patient, but stick to it.

- *Support any small increment of change.* Have a party when he says, "Maybe I *have* had a superior attitude," or when she resentfully gets to work on time. Movement is movement. Affirm him or her. But still stick to it.

Will it work? Of course you can't force anyone to change, but these elements are really God's elements, taken from biblical principles. He designed them to work for all of us.

The Program Can Work if You Work the Program

This approach is not simply a theory, and it's not just guess-work—it's made up of practical approaches that I have seen work many times.

I started this book with the story of a family with a difficult entitlement situation in their home. Now let me tell you the ending. Before we talked, the mom and dad had approached the problem with a combination of feeling guilty, nagging, and angry threats that they didn't follow up on. Their program was definitely not working. We straightened out their approach, based on the principles in this book. Mom and Dad were positive and supportive with their son, but also clear and firm about his entitlement. He did end up having to leave home before he wanted to. But I saw him about a year later. He was working, had his own apartment, and self-respect too. He said, "I needed the push. It wasn't fun, but it made me grow up. I'm where I want to be now."

I have seen this positive result in families with adult children and those with younger children as well. I've seen these principles work in organizations with entitled employees and in friendships where something needs to change. The skills described in this book will help you to make a transformational change in your environment and your relationships. Now join me as, in the rest of the chapters, we examine the practical ways to help the entitled people in your life accept responsibility and accountability.

Skills

1. **Address your own entitlement.** We all have a pocket entitlement of some kind, in some area of life. Work hard and be honest as you identify it. Then take the beam out of your eye—if you're going to ask your friend or relative or employee to do the hard work to rid themselves of the entitlement disease, you have to be willing to do it yourself. Think of the principles and skills we've learned so far. How do they work with you? Which ones have been the most effective? This internal "entitlement audit" will give you an insider's view of the process.

2. **Review your failures so far with that entitled person.** What has gone wrong in your previous attempts to deal with your entitled person? Were you unclear? Did you not follow up? Did you give up in impatience? Did you judge? Identify the attitudes you may need to change.

3. **Be ready to adjust your approach.** Try out the suggestions listed above under "Stick to It" with one of the entitled people you know. Review them with your life team and tweak them. You don't have to do it all right. In fact, with entitlement issues, we always need to be ready to change the play when the situation changes quickly, as it often does. The path isn't set in stone, and every encounter is different. But get engaged and get moving.

CHAPTER 5

MOTIVATION:
WHY DO ALL THIS HARD STUFF, ANYWAY?

THE MOVIE *A LEAGUE OF THEIR OWN* follows the lives of several female professional baseball players during World War II. At one point, a player named Dottie announces that she intends to quit because the job has grown too difficult. Her manager, Jimmy, challenges her decision. He points out how much passion the sport brings into her life. Then he finishes with an unforgettable line about baseball: "It's *supposed* to be hard. If it wasn't hard, everyone would do it. The hard ... is what makes it great."

Do you ever feel like Dottie when it comes to doing hard things? We all do, I imagine. But entitlement *never* likes to face hard things, and if we want to defeat it, Jimmy has something important for us to learn. If you bought this book in order to help you play "Jimmy" in the life of an entitled person, then your challenge is to help him find the motivation he needs to change course and do life the Hard Way.

Anyone who wants to achieve some worthwhile outcome needs to deliberately and intentionally do life the Hard Way — and that takes motivation. Our brains and our bodies scream at us to stop getting up early in the morning, to avoid that difficult conversation, to give up that tough job search. When the screaming starts, we all need some stable foundation to come back to, some bedrock reasons that can help us to keep moving forward. This chapter is designed to help you find that motivation. In fact, you may need to return to this chapter repeatedly as you engage with the entitled people in your life, because when the going gets tough, all of us need strong encouragement to keep going to reach our goals.

Because You Want "Better"

Entitlement whispers at us to take life easy, to pull back, and to chill out. It seduces us with soft words like, "Hey, you're worth it. You don't deserve to have to put in such a hard day." But entitlement and a better life simply don't go together. Like oil and water, they don't mix. Do you want to know the primary and best motivation to do life the Hard Way? Here it is, in all its simplicity:

Your entitled person needs to want better than he has right now.

What kind of "better" do you want in your own life? Lots of things, probably. You don't have to be homeless, broke, and on the street to have a desire for better circumstances. Maybe you want a "better" such as one of the following:

- You want to turn an entry-level job into a career with good growth potential.

- You want to create and own a small business that can provide well for your family.

- You want a satisfying career in which you become best-in-class.

- You want to turn your struggling marriage into a loving union characterized by affection and care.

- You want your "okay" marriage to become more deeply connected and passionate.

- You want a dating life that allows you to find someone who is both a great match and a great connection in your life.

- You want a service or ministry in which you can fulfill your desire to help others, using your talents and gifts to achieve visible results.

- You want to look in the mirror and see a body with more strength, tone, and health.

What *you* want may not appear on this list, but I know at least one thing about you: If you have a pulse, *in some area of your life, you desire better than what you currently have.*

The only exception I can think of is if you're clinically depressed. And in that case, you need to get professional help to reawaken in you a desire for better and a longing for improvement.

Motivated people always feel some sort of discontent, some dissatisfaction, some desire for better. Those feelings, of course, don't usually seem pleasant. In fact, they may feel deeply uncomfortable. But since that feeling of discomfort often drives us toward a better life, it's important to allow ourselves to really *feel* it.

Entitlement makes it all too easy to feel content with mediocrity, to accept something far less than the best, simply because seeking "better" is too hard. The truth is, those who choose to pursue the "better" know from the outset that walking such a road is *not* usually easy.

I was invited by a sports ministry I work with to take my family to the 2014 Super Bowl and speak at one of their events there. After Seattle won, scores of interviewers wanted to talk with the victorious Seahawks players. Over and over, the players described not only their elation at winning the championship, but spoke about getting ready for the hard work of the next season, which they hoped would result in a second championship in 2015. A normal human might think, *Just enjoy this! Next year is a long way off!* But elite athletes aren't wired like that. Even in the euphoria of a victorious locker room, they feel the strong desire to climb the next mountaintop—and that's what drives them to more achievement.

Too often, our inner voice mutes the discomfort of desire:

I'm fine living with my parents.
This job is okay; lots of people have it worse.
At least we don't fight a lot in our marriage.

Statements like that serve as a kind of antidepressant to keep us from feeling the legitimate, God-given desire for better. But it's also important to make a distinction between these "muting desire" statements and the voice of God, who might be saying, "Be content":

> I have learned to be content whatever the circumstances. I know what it is to be in need, and I know what it is to have plenty. I have learned the secret of being content in any and every situation, whether well fed or hungry, whether living in plenty or in want. I can do all this through him who gives me strength. (Philippians 4:11–13)

How do you tell the difference? The best way is: first, surrender — that is, have an open mind to whatever God is saying. Second, be honest about what you are feeling inside. Is it a moment of surrender to God? Or is it about discouragement, fatigue, or fear?

In healthy individuals, there is a gap, a space, between where they are and where they want to be. This gap is what creates and promotes a desire to change.

Consider the person who has no gap. He thinks of himself as perfect, ideal. He has attained everything he thinks is worth attaining. She believes she "has it all together." There's nothing she would change about herself. People like that have no goals or shortcomings — at least in their own minds.

Men or women with this kind of attitude, I have found, usually have to experience difficult losses and relational conflicts before they can wake up to the reality that we *all* have a gap, whether we're aware of it or not. "I thought everything was fine until my kids wouldn't speak to me after they grew up. Only then did I realize how clueless I had been."

In his book *Holy Discontent*, Bill Hybels describes a "firestorm of frustration" that prods us to live more meaningful lives.[5] When you combine that frustration with a desire for better in your own life, you find the motivation to move out of entitlement and live life the hard way. The prescription looks like this:

> *To live the hard way, we must experience the gap*
> *between where you are and where you want to be. And*
> *we must come to believe that dealing with the gap is*
> *our problem and our responsibility.*

As I've said, it's not a pleasant experience; in fact, it can be painful. But there's no other way to defeat entitlement and grasp the better life you really want.

A salesman walked up to the porch of a farmhouse where the farmer was sitting, with his dog lying beside him. The dog was moaning constantly. Concerned, the salesman asked, "Sir, is your dog all right?"

"No," the farmer replied, "he's lying on a tack."

Puzzled, the salesman said, "Then why doesn't he get off the tack?"

"I suppose it doesn't hurt enough yet," answered the farmer.

The dog did have a gap—but not enough of one. His gap felt painful enough to make him moan, but not excruciating enough to motivate him to get him off the tack.

Entitlement will often create negative thoughts to counter our motivation:

- *It's too hard.*

- *You feel satisfied with things as they are.*

- *Just wait for someone else to help you.*

But these thoughts won't help you, either now or in your future.

So don't be afraid of experiencing your desire for better, and don't try to mute your frustration that you aren't there yet. God designed you to want his best, to desire better: "I press on toward the goal to win the prize for which God has called me heavenward in Christ Jesus" (Philippians 3:14).

Because You Need Confidence

Entitlement pushes you to avoid trying, to put out as little effort as possible, so that you never risk failing. Among all the problems of entitlement, one of the most serious is this: *It kills your confidence.* Entitlement saps you of your mojo and robs you of your sense of healthy self-reliance. You want to believe that you have what it takes for this next challenge, but entitlement robs you of that feeling.

Suppose, for instance, you want to become an effective public speaker. You try your luck at a Rotary Club breakfast and recruit your family to show up, to support your first at bat. You speak on success, and although you didn't spend a lot of time preparing, you think it turned out pretty well. Your family tells you, "You were *awesome*, amazing, life changing!" Someone at the breakfast says, "Tony Dungy just cancelled on me for an event I'm hosting at the convention center next week for twenty thousand people. I need you there. You'll be great."

Anyone with good common sense would say, "Thanks for the compliment, but with only one public speech, I'm not ready for prime time yet." You'd say this because it's true. You know that you lack the seasoning and the competence to speak at that level. If you try to do the gig anyway, you risk spectacular failure—hardly a great start to a speaking career. So despite the well-meaning affirmation, you know that you don't yet have the ability. You lack the necessary confidence. Why? *Because confidence is earned, not bequeathed.*

That truth is supported by a wealth of research now coming out about children and entitlement. Scientists are discovering that when kids get overpraised, they become *less* confident and so become risk-averse. Praise is a great thing, and we all need to know that others affirm our efforts and successes. But overpraise is a very different thing. When you overpraise a child, you *affirm successes out of all proportion to reality*—and the child inevitably pays for it. Consider a few everyday examples:

- "Yeah, you struck out. But the pitcher cheated!"—to a kid struggling to figure out which end of the bat to hold.

- "You made an A on the test! You're the smartest kid in the school!"—to a child who knows exactly where she stands on her class's intelligence spectrum—and it isn't at the top.

- "You deserve to be the lead in the play!"—to a child who has only been in one or two plays before and is in awe of the acting ability of his classmates who got the lead roles.

Researchers have found that when kids get overpraised, they know at some level that the praise is not based on reality. So they develop a fear of taking risks and of failing. Most kids have not yet developed the capacity to think, *I know what I'm capable of, and what to do when I come to a situation beyond my capability.* Instead, they overflow with anxiety and shame, and so they just don't try at all.

You're not a kid. But you may be like these kids, at least at some level. Someone may have told you once, "You can do anything you want—just work hard." An inspirational statement—unfortunately, it's just not true. A child can waste a great deal of energy and time on a goal that is impossible for them.

We see evidence of this every night of the week on the current crop of talent competition shows, such as *American Idol* and *The Voice*. In the early rounds, there are always young people who have undoubtedly been overpraised and never gently told they have limited singing talent. The judges will be the first ones in her life to give her a dose of reality. And often, as viewers around the world watch, that reality proves to be devastating for her. Much better for parents to encourage both dreams and hard work and to help their child deal with reality at the same time. It is a difficult balance that defines great parenting.

We all need confidence to win at life, and lots of it. But the only path to great and genuine self-confidence is a history of success. When you can look back at twenty speaking events that went well, or a series of work promotions at the same job, or a year's AA chip, you will feel confident. And you should.

That is the Hard Way.

Confident people don't have to talk themselves into "I can do this." *They know they can, because they already have done it.*

Because a Life of Regret Is Just Awful

A friend of mine got remarried after many years of looking for the right guy. Unfortunately, she wasted a lot of time by first trying a dating strategy that almost never works.

For years, her approach was this: Get quickly super-involved with one guy, date him exclusively in an intense way, start talking about marriage in just a couple of months ... and then feel the pain when the guy finds an excuse to bail out. After each episode, she would feel devastated, take a little time to regroup—and then find another guy to become overinvolved with. She kept this up for about six years.

Finally, she changed her approach. She worked hard to get healthy, built a great support system of women friends, dated several guys at once (but less intensely), didn't become needy, and took her time. Within two years, she got married to a great man.

I asked her to tell me about the path she ultimately took. She said that while she felt happy with how things turned out in the end, she truly regretted the intense, overinvolved years. She had lost a great deal of time. She didn't spiritualize her mistake, as so many people do when they say, "God used it for good." Certainly, God uses lots of things for good, even foolish and unnecessary things. But that doesn't mean that the men and women who do these foolish and unnecessary things don't feel a ton of regret. Lots of great redemptive things happened because of Adam and Eve's fall as described in Genesis 3, but that wasn't God's Plan A.

Regret is a bad feeling, intense and painful. It makes us feel sad and helpless over the hurtful things we wish we had not done or the helpful things we wish we *had* done. We feel helpless because we can't go back in time and do it over, so we must simply learn to live with it. Since we all make mistakes, we all feel some degree of regret.

How does entitlement fit in? It has a consistent way of sowing things today that you will deeply regret tomorrow, or next year, or twenty years from now. And do you really want that?

Regrets can result from nearly anything: not taking a job seriously, failing to save money, remaining a "player" for too long, putting off a relationship with God, eating whatever we want to stuff in our mouths. Ask someone suffering from type 2 diabetes whether they regret their choice of diet in the years leading up to their diagnosis.

I have my own regrets. I wish I had learned to study hard in high school, rather than learning the really hard way in grad school. Diligence early on would have spared me a great deal of trouble in my academic life. I learned from those regrets, and I've grown. Those regrets make me think harder about the choices I make today, because I want as few regrets as possible for the rest of my life. Here's the bottom line: *You minimize regret tomorrow by doing hard things today.*

Because You Were Designed to Achieve Your Potential

One of the greatest experiences humans can have is to know they are reaching their potential in some area of life. Olympic athletes who train and push at incredible levels for many years have peak experiences when they win, experiences that most of us can't imagine. Part of their exhilaration comes from knowing that they are doing what they were designed to do, and at the highest level possible.

Like these elite athletes, you'll seldom be more exhilarated than when you realize you have maximized your potential in some important area.

Some time ago, I began coaching the members of a family-owned business. They were particularly concerned about a young man, a family member, who seemed like "Mr. Potential" but had so far produced no tangible results. He was smart and had great people skills. He was being groomed to help take over the company—but among the family's concerns was that "Mr. Potential" suffered from the disease of entitlement. He didn't have a severe case, maybe a three on a scale of ten, but the illness affected him enough to make him undisciplined, rob him of follow-through skills, and keep him unfocused. His entitlement had told him, "You're a good guy with unlimited potential, and that should be enough."

But it wasn't enough. The company could not depend on him to fulfill his potential. He just didn't have the required performance.

When I discussed it with him in a family meeting, he grew

defensive and immediately wanted to disengage. "You guys don't get it," he said. "Things are fine! You're all just micromanaging."

But I got a different picture when I talked to him alone. He felt miserable and frustrated with himself, though he didn't want his relatives to know. He once broke down in tears, confessing to me, "I'm not getting the job done. I'm a fake." My heart went out to the young man. He clearly suffered from a great deal of private misery.

I began taking the young man through the Hard Way principles that make up the chapter headings in this book. Step-by-step, he began feeling better, relating better, and performing better. Over time, he started taking on higher and higher levels of responsibility within the company. The end result was that he was using more of his potential to achieve and bear fruit. He felt energized, challenged, and confident.

God has designed you, too, with all sorts of potential to be and do things you never thought you could accomplish. He actually *created* you for these matters: "For we are God's handiwork, created in Christ Jesus to do good works, which God prepared in advance for us to do" (Ephesians 2:10). What a statement of potential! You have tremendous good works ahead of you—in your marriage, in your parenting, in your dating life, in your career, and in your mission. It's all part of the Plan.

If you will enter the Hard Way path, you will take your place in God's kingdom as someone firing on all cylinders. And when that happens, you will see life take a dramatic turn for the better.

Because You Want Great Relationships

Entitlement poisons relationships. Who wants to hang around a self-absorbed, entitled person? Who yearns to listen to someone talk about themselves 90 percent of the time, blame fate and other people for their problems, have little interest in taking ownership for personal difficulties, and show little interest in the unlucky man or woman who regularly spends a lot of time with them? I can testify that a lunch hour spent with an entitled individual can feel like an unpleasant year.

Healthy, balanced people just don't put up with such behavior for long. Entitled individuals tend to attract friends who listen forever and innocently hope things will get better on their own, or those who are always trying to give advice and solve problems (call those "helping" relationships), or those who themselves are entitled and whose lives also don't work (call those "fun, let's stay entitled" relationships). Those who are in a "helping" relationship with an entitled person mean well, but the relationship quickly becomes frustrating because nothing ever changes. It is no healthier for the entitled person.

But there's a third category of relationship for the entitled person (and for the rest of us, too): growth relationships. This means peers, friends, mutual strugglers, and equals who are willing to walk down the journey of life, together. At some level, *everyone wants and needs growth relationships*. Relationships which promote growth require the presence of grace and truth in each person, two qualities exemplified by Jesus himself (John 1:14). For both individuals, this means accepting each other's frailties and hurts while continuing to challenge each other to grow, change, and get better. The entitled person generally knows that the "helping" relationship makes him or her into a dependent child—a painful position to be in and one that erodes the small amount of self-respect that may yet exist. The "fun, let's stay entitled" relationship becomes a permanent party that feels good for a time, but that bears no real and substantive fruit. In fact, over time it deteriorates and degrades the life of both individuals trapped in it.

I was working with a man in his late twenties who had been

described as a classic slacker. He still lived at home, showed little ambition, and Mom and Dad paid all his expenses (though they regularly nagged him to get his life together, a habit that kept everyone miserable). Eventually they asked for help. The young man wasn't excited about trying to change his life, but he did know at some level that he didn't respect himself and that his perpetual party relationships were getting him nowhere. (This is not, by the way, the same family I described in chapter 1. The case of entitlement in this family was not as severe as in the earlier example. But frankly, the situation is common enough that I could cite several other cases from my own experience that would, on the surface, sound nearly identical.)

As we addressed the young man's problem behaviors, he cooperated—he began developing different habits and made gradual lifestyle changes. Eventually, he discovered that he was a talented numbers guy, great with finances. He got training, found a good job, and finally got his own apartment. Sometime later, he told me about an encounter with his old friends: "It was really weird. They were actually boring. Same old parties and stories. Their lives were a dead end. I even felt sorry for them. I think I need some new friends." He wasn't disrespecting his friends. He truly cared about them. But they weren't providing the support and challenge he needed to continue growing and moving for-ward in life. He was moving from the empty calories of a steady diet of fun and good times to the substantive nutrients of interests in growth, responsibility, and achievement.

The Hard Way will draw you to healthy and balanced people who are fun, who respect you, who accept you, and who will also push you when you need it. These people will become gold to you. In fact, great relationships may be the best and highest motivation of all to give up entitlement.

Because the Benefits Far Outweigh the Negatives

At the end of the day, vibrant, satisfying life and entitlement simply don't mix. A life of entitlement is not *supposed* to work, just as no one should feel good while suffering from a bacterial infection. When a nasty bug attacks you, you are *supposed* to feel feverish, fatigued, and achy. It's the pain that drives you to take care of the infection.

Think of entitlement as the disease and the Hard Way as the cure. The Hard Way works—things get better, and your infection goes away.

But not overnight. Entitlement is a tough disease to eradicate. Its cure may require you to take many kinds of "antibiotics." Consider each chapter in this book as a uniquely potent antibiotic designed to target a specific aspect of the illness. As you add each medicine, you will find that life, in all its dimensions, will unfold for you in a great way: "Now to [God] who is able to do immeasurably more than all we ask or imagine, according to his power that is at work within us, to him be the glory of the church and in Christ Jesus throughout all generations, for ever and ever! Amen" (Ephesians 3:20–21).

CHAPTER 6

DISCIPLINE AND STRUCTURE:

MORE DOABLE THAN YOU THINK

A FRIEND OF MINE NAMED DALE lost about fifty pounds and kept it off for a year. After I congratulated him on his accomplishment, I said, "I work with people all the time who can't accomplish this sort of thing. So what's your secret sauce?"

"Discipline," he replied.

I waited for more, then said, "That's it?"

"Yes. I chose discipline."

I hear this a lot from high-performing individuals, and it is always a red flag of interest for me. "That's great," I said. "How did you choose discipline?"

"Well," Dale said, "I was sick of the weight. Sick of feeling crummy, of my clothes not fitting, of being worried about my health. And Marie [his wife] was all over me to lose the weight."

"Sounds like lots of motivation," I said. "So when you chose discipline, did you just wake up the next day and choose the right foods and start working out?"

"Of course not," he replied. "I had no idea what a good regimen would be. I went to see a nutritionist about the food, and I got a gym membership with a trainer. They gave me information and helped me with a plan."

I nodded. "And did you talk to anyone supportive about this, or just do it all on your own?"

"Sure, I talked to people," Dale said. "I asked my men's group to call me and check in on my progress, and Marie helped me stay on track."

"Okay," I said. "Ever fall off the wagon? Get discouraged, get tired of it, bring home stress from work, and go out and eat a bunch of pizzas?"

107

"Sure, at first. It was pretty hard in the first few months, a lot of old habits to quit. My friend and my wife would talk me off the ledge, help me find the triggers, let me know they didn't think I was a loser, and help me get back on the wagon. Eventually the new behaviors became habits, and I didn't need the support as often anymore."

"Sounds like you did everything right," I said. "Congratulations again. But, Dale, you didn't 'choose discipline.'"

"I *did* choose discipline," he said. "I got up early and went to the gym and laid off the snacks. That's discipline."

"No, *you underwent a process of discipline,* and then you *became* a disciplined person. It wasn't some simple 'just do it' choice. It was a set of experiences you underwent that gave you these new habits."

He didn't look as though he got my point, so I used a metaphor: "When your son Stevie was six, how long could he last doing his homework? He's sitting at the kitchen table doing addition and subtraction. Could he go an hour at a stretch?"

"Are you kidding?" Dale replied. "At that age, Stevie couldn't go ten minutes, and if we went longer, he would get squirrelly or he'd have a meltdown."

"Right," I said. "My kids were the same way. Now that Stevie is in grad school, how long can he study?"

"He did an all-nighter last week. Hours and hours."

"Impressive," I said. "So why didn't you tell him at six years old to 'choose discipline'? 'Just choose several hours at the kitchen table, little Stevie.' Wouldn't that have saved you and Marie a lot of time?"

"Well," Dale sighed, "he couldn't have done it."

"It wasn't a choice?"

"No. It wasn't a choice he could make. There is no way he could have chosen that. He was just six years old."

"Okay," I said, "so what happened to get Stevie from ten minutes at age six to hours and hours at age twenty-four?"

"Marie and I did a lot of things," Dale answered. "We used egg timers, we supervised, we encouraged him, we found out what his range was, the teachers helped us, we increased it by a bit every month, we gave him consequences and rewards."

And then the lights came on.

"And . . . that is what I did to lose the weight, too," he said.

"Yes," I agreed. "You received discipline in a process, and it became part of you. You didn't 'choose discipline.' You chose a path that disciplined you."

Dale nodded his head. "I get it," he replied. "Stevie and I got the help and the discipline came."

Dale did get it. He was doing a lot of right things with himself, just as he'd done a lot of right things with Stevie. But the process didn't get the credit.

You Need Discipline in Just About Everything Important

If you want to succeed in life, career, relationships, or health, you will need discipline. There really is no option. The habit of discipline will help you create great habits, day after day and year after year. Discipline creates a great company out of a small garage, an intimate, long-term marriage out of a glance at a party, a movie that fascinates millions out of an idea shared over dinner, a church that sends God's love to other continents out of a neighborhood Bible study. Discipline turns a first-grade exposure to intriguing new subject matter into a graduate degree.

Discipline is goal oriented. It harnesses your energy so that you don't get distracted, so that you become productive. When you combine discipline with innovation and the right values, you can accomplish what amount to miracles in your life and for the world.

Disciplined people don't have to be rigid, anal-retentive types, or authoritarian control freaks. (And when they are, it usually means that something else is going wrong.) Some of the most enjoyable people in my life have strong discipline. They really can be nice, relaxed, fun people. They just do the right things on a regular basis, over and over again — whether they feel like it or not. That's how they come out winners.

Disciplined people are patient. They know that their behaviors are part of a process on the way to an important goal. If your goal is just to do whatever you wanted to do, and to do it right now, you would not need discipline. But losing lots of weight, having great relationships, finding your career niche, and being successful all take time, and they involve delaying gratification repeatedly over the course of that time.

Many people get so frustrated about themselves that they don't develop the discipline to save money, lose weight, have a regular devotional time, learn a language, train for a new career, or learn new relational skills. They give up too quickly, and then have an even harder time believing that they are capable of accomplishing great things.

Entitlement: The Anti-Discipline

Many of our failures in discipline have their roots in the current entitlement culture that surrounds us. Consider two common entitlement mantras regarding discipline, and two Hard Way mantras that counteract them. (You'll find frequent references throughout the book to entitlement mantras and Hard Way mantras. Pay special attention to those comparisons — they provide a quick and concise statement of the way the harmful attitudes of entitlement differ from the healthier attitudes of the Hard Way.)

The first entitlement mantra declares: *I shouldn't have to be a disciplined person. I'm above all that; I don't need it.* Individuals who live by this mantra don't see value in hard work, incremental behavioral changes, and patience. They believe they can be happy without being disciplined. Maybe they're good with people and think their relational skills are enough to get them through life. Or perhaps they think their intelligence will do the trick. Or they feel so unmotivated to accomplish *anything* that the effort and self-denial of discipline don't seem worth it.

The Hard Way mantra takes exactly the opposite tack. It says: *Discipline will help me achieve what matters. It is the engine that drives my dreams, my vision, and my goals.* This mantra reminds us that some structure — schedules, accountability, measureable goals, rules — is necessary if you're going to accomplish what you hope to accomplish. Success comes to those who work at it, and whose work is not just determined but disciplined.

The second entitlement mantra is even less healthy than the first: *If I have to be disciplined, then I should be able to be disciplined right now.* Dale started out that way. He put way too much faith in his ability to choose the right thing. Until we talked about Stevie, he thought all you had to do was decide to be disciplined.

The Hard Way mantra looks different: *Discipline requires an external support structure, over time.* Dale was smart enough to not try to go it on his own; he relied on his wife and his men's group to cheer him on and keep him honest. Those who care enough about their goals to be determined to succeed in their discipline will likewise build a support structure of their own.

Although these two entitlement attitudes have become popular in our culture, following them leads to failure, regret, and heartbreak. In this chapter, I'll present the underlying nature of discipline (it's not what you think!) and explain how you can make it part of your life forever.

The OS That Drives the Discipline App

As we saw in Dale's story, the skill of discipline is based on a process of information and support that works over time. This process creates and develops a critical character ability that psychologists call *internal structure*. Internal structure is the capacity to focus your energy over time. It is the steady framework of your mind. Internal structure is a combination of your capacities to focus, persevere, and delay gratification toward a goal. Just as your skeleton is the structure of your body, protecting and strengthening your organs, so internal structure protects and strengthens your goals and makes possible your very survival.

When you get distracted or find yourself under stress, bored, or discouraged, internal structure keeps you on track and on target. Individuals who enjoy solid internal structure can discipline themselves at an effective level. They set and keep goals, have great long-term habits, and get life done. Those without good internal structure have difficulty holding steady for what they desire over time.

Discipline is the app, and internal structure is the operating system that drives the app. Discipline rests on, and is driven by, internal structure. Internal structure also supports other important apps, such as patience, delay of gratification, frustration tolerance, and goal-oriented behavior. If the structure doesn't exist, the app will never work. All the "I've got to be strong" statements, all the New Year's resolutions, and all the "I am choosing discipline" mantras will break down and fail you—if you lack a strong internal structure.

I love time management information. I read the books and

attend the seminars. There's always something helpful for me and my clients, such as David Allen's two-minute rule: "If an action will take less than two minutes, it should be done at the moment it is defined."[6] That simple principle changed my life in getting my day organized.

But all the time-management systems in the world won't make you a disciplined, effective person if you lack internal structure. That's one reason people get discouraged with such systems. They get discouraged either with themselves, because they conclude that they aren't really serious about success, or with the management system, because they feel that the system somehow failed them. Most likely, neither is true. These individuals simply didn't have a strong enough "skeleton" to consistently follow through on the principles and tips.

This also explains why a lot of weight-loss and self-help programs don't work for many people. The programs fail because they are often based on the "discipline is a choice" idea. Those who have lots of internal structure may well succeed in those programs, despite their flaws. But many people completely lack it, so for them, the rah-rah approach fails over time.

How Internal Structure Grows

So how do you develop internal structure?

You do so through a process psychologists call "internalization." We internalize something when we "take in" an experience and it becomes part of who we are. Internalization is more than learning a list or memorizing a procedure; it involves both thinking and experiencing over time.

When you spend a lot of time with a music teacher, for example, you learn notes and chords. You repeatedly go over scales and songs. And over time, you internalize the lessons. They become second nature; you can make use of them without conscious thought.

Internalization drives all business training. When I am doing management training, I often do a content piece on how to motivate teams, using several principles and illustrations. Then I do a skill-building segment where the attendees try out the new skills on each other. As they internalize these experiences, the new skills become part of their leadership skill sets forever.

Dale internalized the experiences of spending time with his nutritionist, his trainer, and his training schedule. These new behaviors became habits that now work for him. In a similar way, Dale and Marie provided external structure (I'll explain this important term more fully a few paragraphs below) for Stevie. Their external structure was their attention, the schedule they set up, and the rewards and consequences program they created to help him. He had little ability to study when he was six, either neurologically, cognitively, or emotionally. But their help, over time, gave him the discipline that eventually he made part of himself. Stevie no longer needs his parents to set egg timers or give him an extra dessert. The ability to study is now part of his own internal wiring.

Several aspects of successful internalization, which creates solid internal structure, form the essential ingredients that allow it to work:

1. *A worthwhile goal.* Internal structure works best when you're pursuing something that matters to you, whether it be health, finances, spiritual growth, dating, or marriage. If it is important to you—if it's worth it—you become more willing to enter the process of internalization.

There's a term I use to help define structure: *cross-context.* What this means is that, if you achieve some success in one area, the habits that enabled you to achieve that success will transfer to other areas as well. Learning to work out, for example, can lead to learning to have great and meaningful devotionals. The contexts cross over.

2. *An external structure.* An external structure is a framework of reminders and short-term goals that breaks time down into bite-sized elements. For example:

- Couples set up a budget system to help buy a new home.

- An athlete develops a training program featuring race-time increments.

- A CEO has a strategic path to go IPO in five years.

- A man who wants to lose weight has an app that measures his food intake, based on his goals.

External structure must also have a *calendarized process.* That is, things work best when they get put in a calendar, where you regularly see them. For example: setting weekly times to have networking meetings; having a date night with your spouse; working out. Don't give up on the calendarized aspect. Allow yourself time to get it to work.

You tend to accomplish what you calendar. We are busy people. If it's a good idea and you'll get to it "one day," you probably won't. When I am working on a particular area of growth, I will give myself sixty days of calendaring it, when I literally input the activity on my physical calendar. Sometimes this happens when I am deep within a book project; at other times it relates to getting enough sleep; and sometimes it involves some spiritual activity.

Just as a cast encases a broken arm and functions to keep the arm straight, as an unbroken bone would do, so external structure gives us protection and strength when we lack what it takes to discipline ourselves in some area. Then, when the bone gets strong, we remove the cast.

3. *Relational support.* The external frame is not enough. We also need supportive and accepting people to help us develop internal structure. Relationships serve as the anesthetic that helps us get through the surgery of developing internal structure. It can be painful to learn a new habit or to become a disciplined person! Discipline can get repetitive, boring, and hard — and the distractions never end. Not only that, but the judge in our mind beats us up and prompts us to think of ourselves as losers. *I'll never get it right,* we think.

You need a life team of people whom you recruit for the specific goal of helping you create internal structure. To qualify for this role, they must have three characteristics:

- *They accept you as you are, with no judgment.* They can't have an ounce of condemnation or harsh judgmentalism. You have to be able to fail and confess, over and over again, and experience love and acceptance from them. Otherwise, you will end up avoiding being vulnerable with them, or sabotaging the process for yourself.

- *They encourage and push you when you need it.* A good life team member loves you as you are, but loves you enough to help you not stay the way you are. These team members aren't mean, but they do nudge you when you get distracted, lazy, or out of focus.

- *They are engaged in growth.* You have a real edge when your life team is made up of people who refuse merely to sit in the stands, observing, but who continue to work on themselves as well. They identify with your efforts and struggles, and they can speak from experience.

Personal growth comes from internalizing not only the external structure, but also your life team's relational warmth. When this happens, the emotional memories of good people live inside you, encouraging you for the rest of your life, keeping you loved and grounded: "being rooted and established in love" (Ephesians 3:17). An added component is how a life team makes growth and success about *us*, not just *me*. You are part of a community that you serve, as it serves you. You may even find yourself on the life team of one of your supporters.

4. *Information and expertise.* You always need the kind of information that can accelerate your internalization process. Dale had a nutritionist and a trainer. You may want to google information on careers, jobs, financial help, or relationships. Become an information junkie. I am one, and it has always paid off for me in my growth.

When you combine these four ingredients, good things happen. The system works if you work the system!

Don't forget that while developing internal structure is hard work, it is still *relational* work. As you work on structure, you should remember that you are not alone. You are not alone from your supportive relationships, and you are not alone from God himself. In fact, one way to translate the word "discipline" in the New Testament is "nurture," as in Hebrews 12:5: "My son, do not make light of the Lord's [nurture]." When we experience and internalize God's nurture in his process of growth, our internal structure grows and flourishes. As a result, discipline, and then goal achievement, occur. That is at the heart of Hard Way living.

Structure Boot Camp

Finding yourself discouraged about your frustrations and failures in several areas of life can feel overwhelming. You may think of yourself as a loser on all levels, with not one healthy area of life where you can feel good about yourself.

When I have a client in this situation, sometimes I create a Structure Boot Camp (SBC) for the person. SBC is an intensive training process that covers multiple areas, designed to shock the system (just like military boot camp) so that the person quickly experiences hope in a general way about all major aspects of life. You can easily set up your own version of SBC for yourself using my description below.

To design an SBC, I have the client list all areas of frustration: marriage, spiritual health, emotional health, parenting, finances, career, and physical health, for example. We then develop goals for all of them. We set up the system using the four aspects of internalization: goals, external structure, support, and information.

The key is that *the client has to prune everything that isn't absolutely necessary—for ninety days.* Postpone family vacation. Don't start a new business. Don't sign up to be an elder in the church. Don't move to a new home. Don't get pregnant. You can do all of that later. The idea is to put all available energy into the boot camp, which has to consume your life for three months. It doesn't matter if your friends get tired of you talking about it; they just have to support you for the length of the camp. You have to invest yourself completely, to the point of obsession, for those ninety days. It has to be that way to change your neural pathways and your habits.

Your life team should have a copy of all targeted areas and all goals. They schedule calls and texts so that every twenty-four hours, you get a brief, encouraging contact from one person. Your life team holds a small celebration for you at thirty and sixty days and a large one at ninety.

This is when cross-context really takes over. One executive I took through the process told me that, a year later, he feels more "automatic" about his good habits. In other words, these habits don't require a lot of psyching himself up, overcoming dread, or even effort. They have become part of who he is inside; they've become as normal as turning on the TV or walking to the refrigerator. The new internal structure has created the discipline he needs.

Obstacles Ahead

You *will* encounter problems as you work on your internal structure. Don't let this discourage you; it only makes sense. Whatever kept you from having internal structure in the first place hasn't gone away. So take stock of the major obstacles and consider what you can do about them.

- *Isolation.* If you've read this book so far, I'm sure you've picked up on this as a major theme: Don't try to do it all on your own, without support. Some people go the loner route because of serious trust issues, some have developed people-pleasing habits that drain them, and some nurture a grandiose sense of their own self-sufficiency. Don't get caught in the isolation trap. Be humble enough to ask for support; people will probably feel happy to help. Don't be like the successful executive I worked with who, in his early sixties, told me, "I have accomplished a lot. But I could have accomplished so much more if I had been vulnerable and let people support me."

- *Life problems.* Don't wait for life to get easy. For 99.999 percent of us, it won't ever be perfectly easy. If you wait for that moment, you may end up solving crises forever and never get to your goals. Go ahead and start the program to develop internal structure *now*—unless the house is on fire, you are going bankrupt, or you have a child suffering from a serious medical condition. Move ahead with your program, and you'll find that your perspective will become healthier and the problems that have kept you away from your own life will finally leave room for you.

- *Extremism:* This is the tendency to be highly enthusiastic and intense about your growth, to the point of going completely gonzo — then at some point (usually quickly) becoming discouraged and burning out. In this process, an "all or nothing" mentality never works. This is one of the primary reasons that people go on dozens of diets that don't work, change jobs often, have serial relational problems, and endure great struggles in finances. If you have an extremist mentality, the little voice in your head is demanding that you get everything fixed and okay *right now.* Say good-bye to that attitude. The truth is, you will struggle and fail more than once on the journey to accomplishing your goals. At the same time, recognize that you will have to continue to drive to work, go see movies, and take it easy during the process. Don't be a sprinter; be in it for the long run. No more yo-yo self-improvement!

- *Self-judgment.* When you experience lapses in discipline and you act out with potato chips, oversleeping, TV, Facebook, or alcohol, your inner judge will attack you and try to convince you how bad you are. A harsh inner judge can totally derail the structuring process. If you are vulnerable to this judge, you need to have your life team speak to your failures, *not your successes.* This is where grace makes a difference. Instead of them telling you, "You didn't really screw up; it wasn't a big deal," ask them to be honest — as when they say, "You did screw up. It was a big deal. But I like you and I'm not mad at you. I'll help you." Grace for our failures neutralizes self-judgment so that we can fight another day.

- *Triggers.* Disruptive events can throw us off and set us back a week or two in learning structure. Figure out the ones you're vulnerable to and prepare for them. A few examples:

  Boredom

  Not seeing results fast enough

  Someone who feels upset with you

  A temporary relapse

  Friends who want you to drop your structure and go play with them

  Someone who asks for your time and energy, even when you don't have it to give

We have to expect and address disrupters like these. But don't let them get you off track! Be loving and caring, but also read *Boundaries* by Henry Cloud and me.[7] It will help you say no when you need to.

Those Who Go Cold Turkey

A friend with whom I discussed the contents of this chapter told me, "I have a son who was heavy into drugs. His life was going down the tubes. Four years ago, he saw what the drugs were doing to him, and he stopped cold turkey. He's been drug free since then. He has had no counseling, no AA meetings, support structures, growth groups, rehab, or church involvement. And although I would like him to grow spiritually, he has a pretty normal, balanced life. How do you figure him?"

A few people *can* just "choose discipline," because they already have the necessary internal structure in place—even if it seems obscured for a time by conflict. In this case, the young man had good family upbringing, consistent love and limits, and developed a good work ethic. So when he got involved in drugs, his structure just got stored in a parking lot in the back of his mind. When he realized he didn't like the turn his life was taking, he simply reactivated his structure.

Unfortunately, people like him are in the great minority. Most of us don't have this capacity. We would like to believe we are like him, and we may try to convince ourselves that we are. But for the vast majority of us, down that way lies failure. Better far to get into this growth process and find out for sure!

Stay the Course

If anything I've said in this chapter sounds discouraging, let me encourage you instead. While it's hard to create discipline at first, it gets easier later. It doesn't stay as boring, or discouraging, or frustrating as it might seem at first. You, or the entitled person you're helping, begin over time to feel more hope and self-respect. I have seen the material in this chapter alone help so many people help others who are living in entitlement, by helping them learn discipline. Living the Hard Way is just what its name suggests — hard. But it helps you create the internal structure you need to stay the course and achieve your goals.

Skills

1. **Meditate on Proverbs 21:5**: "The plans of the diligent lead to profit as surely as haste leads to poverty." Ask God to help you have a profitable life, in all senses of the word, by diligently following through on your plans.

2. **Keep your goals physically present.** Individuals, couples, businesses, and churches need to see their goals before their eyes, several times a week. Put them on your

smartphone Notes app, on the walls of your factory plant, and on your refrigerator. We all need reminders. God taught his people to keep his laws physically before them (see Deuteronomy 6:6−9), connected to them, to help them stay encouraged and focused.

3. **Begin with small steps and quick gratification.** Baby steps work when you're starting the process. If keeping up with your blog is your goal, then write your blog for thirty minutes before doing Facebook for ten (never make the gratification longer or more expensive than the desired behavior). Have the hard conversation you've been avoiding, then have lunch with a person who loves you and is fun. Gradually extend yourself as the habits become more internalized.

4. **If you are still failing and discouraged.** This happens often, so relax—you are normal. It generally means you need some combination of three things: amping up the relational support (double the contacts); creating more structure (daily goals instead of weekly); or getting counseling (to resolve an internal issue that is sabotaging the process).

CHAPTER 7

CREATE A SELF-IMAGE THAT ACTUALLY HELPS YOU

A LARGE COMPANY hired me to work with one of its executives. Starting some diagnostics to develop a path to help him perform better, I said, "So tell me about your strength areas and problem areas."

He immediately corrected me. "It's better to talk about strengths and growth opportunities," he said.

"You like the term *growth opportunities* better than *problem areas*?" I asked.

"Yes. There are no problems, there are only opportunities."

I pressed a bit. "So, problems don't exist?"

The executive smiled and replied, "I think it's better to think of them as opportunities. The term *problems* seems negative."

I nodded. "Yes, the word *problem* means something negative is happening. But what's wrong with stating a negative reality?"

"It is just demoralizing," he said. "And I don't want to feel that way when I lead my division."

"I get that," I said. "No one wants to feel bad while they're leading the troops. But what if you came to the doctor with a temperature and chills and he said, 'I don't want to be negative and tell you that you have a bacterial infection. Let's just be positive about this'?"

He thought a moment and answered, "I get it. Okay, what are my problems as a leader?"

"You have a lot of strengths, first off," I said. "You are clear in your vision and your path. And you like your people, you truly do. But you're too harsh with them."

Instantly he reverted to his old ways: "I'm not really harsh; I'm just a very direct person."

"You're doing it again," I said. "I've seen you dress people down in this office, and it's not about directness. You lose your warmth, and you really are too tough on them."

He had a hard time accepting my observation; he actually felt proud of his directness. But I kept making a distinction between direct and harsh, and eventually the lights started coming on.

I gave him some coaching homework assignments to do over the next couple of months — practices that directed him to use kinder tones and words while staying direct with his people. Over time, he became a much more effective boss as his direct reports responded to his newfound warmth.

Let's review what happened. My client was and is a good person and a very good leader. He has done well in his sector. But the culture of entitlement had infected him and shaped how he looked at himself. For a time, he resisted the possibility that he might "have a problem" and instead insisted he had only "opportunities."

The truth is that I have never worked with a highly successful person who continued to resist reality. The mega-achievers always want to know what might be wrong about them and what might be right about them — and they don't flinch.

Your self-image is important. How you experience yourself can make all the difference between success and failure, between entitlement and Hard Way living.

Your self-esteem can bring clarity. It can make you confident. It can also set you up terribly when you face challenges.

Is your self-image working for you and your goals and your life, or against you? Your "report card on yourself," which is what self-image basically is, makes a huge difference.

Playing Word Games

In this area of self-image, the entitlement culture has done a great deal of damage. The culture tells us to avoid looking at anything negative about ourselves and look only at the positive, because a negative observation might deflate us and make us feel bad about ourselves. So we play word games, which can become patently contrived:

- A lack of timeliness becomes "free spiritedness."

- An inability to follow through becomes "spontaneity."

- A tendency to blame others for one's failures becomes "spinning a lot of plates."

- Inability to keep promises becomes "a lack of rigidity and black-and-white thinking."

We do all of this semantic arm-twisting so that we won't feel bad. While I am no proponent of people feeling bad, here's the issue: *If our self-image doesn't allow us to mention problems, we have no possibility for improvement.* Which means we are stuck with what we are. Since free spiritedness, spontaneity, spinning plates, and not being rigid are not problems to solve, we have nowhere to go.

And our doctor never gives us the antibiotics we need.

The Antibiotic of Sober Judgment

The Bible has a healthier and more helpful view of self-image than the culture of entitlement provides. It's pretty simple.

First, we are to have "sober judgment" about ourselves. That is, we are to be realistic and not just blow smoke to make ourselves feel good:

For by the grace given me I say to every one of you: Do not think of yourself more highly than you ought, but rather think of yourself with sober judgment, in accordance with the faith God has distributed to each of you. (Romans 12:3)

That means admitting it—and not being afraid to call it what it is—when you see negatives: "I am sometimes lazy." "I am too hard on myself." "I avoid difficult things." "I am afraid to let people down." *Now* there is something to fix, heal, and transform.

This doesn't mean that everything negative my self-image says about me is true. Lots of people have suffered from harsh self-images that need to be corrected and clarified. Self-statements such as "I am unlovable" or "I am worthless" are not only untrue, but they are obstacles in your ability to grow, to be healthy, and to become successful. Those are false negatives. But a true negative identifies a problem to address.

Second, you are to own what is positive about you. If God made a good trait in you, remember that he doesn't make mistakes: "I praise you because I am fearfully and wonderfully made; your works are wonderful, I know that full well" (Psalm 139:14). It is not pride or arrogance to be happy and praise God because he created good things in you. Feeling good about all that helps you to develop these strengths to their fullest and then use these positive aspects to make the world a better place. For example, you may have:

- The capacity to love deeply

- A high value for holiness and God's ways

- Empathy for others

- The ability to work hard and be diligent

- The knack of accepting the imperfections of others and yourself

This is the mixed bag of a healthy self-image: seeing and using the positive in you, and seeing and improving the negative in you.

Over dinner with a married couple with whom we were friends, the wife started talking about how overwhelming and exhausting her schedule felt, with kids, church involvements, and some friends in crisis who demanded her time and energy. I felt deep concern for her, as we had had the exact same conversation a year earlier, with no apparent improvement.

"I'm worried about you burning out, and you can't afford to with your young kids," I said. "What do you think is driving all this exhaustion and over-involvement?"

"I think I just love too much," she replied.

"Sorry," I answered, "but I totally disagree with that."

She looked at me askance. I imagine that most of her friends had probably told her, "Yes, and what a big heart you have," or something to that effect.

But I wanted her to get better!

"It's impossible to 'love too much,'" I explained. "There is no way. I mean, God himself is love (1 John 4:8). The more we love, the better life should be. I think it's not that you love too much, but that you set limits too little. You don't say no when you need to, you tend to enable people, and you do things that others should be doing. I would hope for you that you would try saying no more, which means letting people down, and dealing with the fears you have about letting them down. I bet you'll feel a lot better in a few weeks, and you won't have to worry about finding a way to love people less."

Her husband nodded in agreement. "That makes sense to me, too! I love how caring you are, so don't make that the villain here. Make your fear of letting others down the problem."

My friend took the challenge, and today she is much more

balanced. Although she's still busy, she's no longer headed toward burnout.

Do you see the difference? Her "I am such a loving person" self-image got in the way of the real issue: "I am scared to say no."

The Double Self-Image Problem of Entitlement

God designed your self-image to be your friend and ally, to help you make great choices, to find your passions, and to succeed in all walks of life. And it was designed also to help you *fail well*. This is one of your self-image's greatest benefits. You need to learn to fail in healthy and redemptive ways, because fail you will.

People with a healthy and accurate self-image don't have a big problem with failure. When they don't get a promotion at work, or their spouse gets mad at them, or their kids don't respect them, they know what to do. Here's what failure looks like when our healthy self-image enables us to fail well:

- *Disappointment:* That was a bummer; I'm sad about this.

- *Leaning on God:* I need his help and wisdom in this.

- *Support:* I think I need to call my friend Pat about this and get some face time.

- *Learning:* What was my contribution to this problem? What do I need to change?

- *Adaptation:* It's time to swing the bat again and try things a different way.

That's how it *should* work when we fail. Since failure, and even repeated failure, is simply a given in life, then over and over again we go through these five steps, and each next time we fail well and at a higher level.

Entitlement cripples your ability to fail well and hampers your capacity to learn and grow from failure. Research has shown that entitlement creates a paradox of self-images within us, one external and the other internal. The two self-images are in conflict.

The person with entitlement looks confident about himself on the outside, to the point of arrogance or cockiness. He doesn't need to prepare his talk, practice his golf swing, or take a course on building a resume. His external self-image says, "I am above all that because I am special."

Given what we've seen and experienced about entitlement, we might expect this. What we might not expect is that there exists a different self-image deeper within the entitled person, one that is insecure and afraid, *and above all, risk-averse.* The entitled person is deathly afraid of taking a risk and failing. The risk he's avoiding might be asking out the goddess he has been worshiping from afar, or applying for the dream job, or asking a friend to hang out with him who might just say no. In all cases, the perceived failure would be too devastating. So he postures about his specialness, but he never gets anywhere because he remains frozen in his ability to take normal risks that everyone has to endure to get anywhere. His internal self-image says, "I can't do this and I can't try."[8]

I have a friend whose parents encouraged him in what he was gifted at and could do easily but avoided pushing him in areas he would have to work hard in to be successful. He was a talented musician but didn't like math. So they let him slide in math and kept him focused on music. The result? As an adult, he loves his music, but he has great difficulty in his financial life and has been in serious trouble with his money. So does he face his financial challenges? No, he freezes and avoids them, because he is so overwhelmed when dealing with matters that are hard for him. After all, dealing with difficult matters is a skill his parents never forced him to learn while young. You don't want your child, spouse, or employee to have this experience.

There is one simple solution to this "double self-image" problem: *Help people to feel competent because they are competent.* The young baseball player doesn't need groundless praise; he needs parents and coaches who will support his attempts to develop a better swing with hundreds of pitched balls until he starts connecting. The young grad student needs a job where she is around people as intelligent as she is, who challenge her and who help her wrestle with difficult matters.

People don't first feel competent and then *become* competent. It's the other way around. They become competent and *then* they feel competent. It is the history, the experience, the at-bats, that create a sense of "I can do this." And before we reach that point, all we have is, "I have people who love and support me while I am not-yet-competent." And that is enough. The sequence, then, is this:

1. Before you achieve competence, you are loved, you are okay, you are supported by God and others. It is grace, the essence of love that is not performance-based: "Though I am not competent at this, I am loved" is the positive self-image at this stage.

2. You try new things, and while no one does them well at first, the "loved" self-image carries the day.

3. You practice, learn, get advice, fail, and adapt.

4. *Gradually,* you begin doing things better. Now the self-image says, "I am loved, *and* I am competent."

This is what *works.* Love precedes confidence, but confidence can't exist outside of failure and adaptation. When your self-image aligns with what is real and true about you—in other words, *how God sees and experiences you*—it works *for* you and not *against* you.

Skills

Here are a few skills to help you develop the self-image that will take you through hard times into success and a healthy lifestyle. Try these on yourself, or with someone who needs help with self-image issues.

1. **Create a simple self-image table with four columns:** True Positives, True Negatives, False Positives, and False Negatives. Without thinking extensively about it, list five aspects of how you see yourself, or have seen yourself, in each column. For example, in True Positives, you might list "Patient with others." In True Negatives, "Get distracted when things get difficult." In False Positives, "Think I am better than others sometimes." And in False Negatives, "Think I am hopeless when I make a mistake." Concentrate on maximizing what is true rather than what is false, *even if it is negative.* Negative reality is more powerful than positive nonreality.

2. **Meditate on Psalm 139 and Romans 3,** two passages that define the range of self-image. Psalm 139 is about how wonderful a creation we are; Romans 3, about our tendency to go our own way and forget who God is. Ask God to help you see yourself as both, and to help you grasp that he loves and can handle both aspects of yourself.

3. **Ask three safe people in your life to look at your list from #1.** Ask them their impressions of the contents

of your four columns. Once they have given their input, ask them if they are okay with your True Positives and True Negatives. Then ask them whether, even assuming the True Negatives continue, they will stick with you in the relationship. Some friends are hesitant about this part because they want to insist on rescuing us from those negatives. But tell them, "I am in a course of self-improvement and growth. The only way I can be the person I need to be is to have good friends who will be honest about my failings and help me improve. I'm not fragile."

CHAPTER 8

CHANGE "I DESERVE" TO "I AM RESPONSIBLE"

AN ELEMENTARY SCHOOL in the city where one of my sons, Ricky, attended college asked me to speak at a parents' event on the topic of raising healthy kids in an entitled culture. Leaving for the airport to fly to the engagement, I called Ricky and explained where I would be speaking that night. "Look," I said. "The parents would probably rather hear from you than me on this topic. After all, you're the 'end product' of everything I'll be talking about tonight, and they'll be curious. Would you come tonight and speak for five minutes on how we parented you in this entitled culture?" He agreed.

When I landed, I drove to the school and presented my talk. The parents in attendance, clearly anxious about how to resource and provide for their kids without spoiling them, were engaged and had questions such as: What if, at age nine, their kids didn't get a cell phone even though their classmates got one? Would that damage their self-esteem and their relationships?

I stressed that Barbi and I had told our kids in a thousand ways, "As you go through life with us, you will need a lot of things. You'll get what you need—things like love, food, shelter, safety, values, structure, faith, opportunity, and an education. We are committed to seeing that you get what you need. But we also want you to know that you really don't *deserve* anything. You can't demand a toy, a phone, a laptop, or a car. That attitude won't work with us. Need, yes; deserve, not so much." The parents seemed to respond positively to my counsel.

Toward the end of my presentation, I saw Ricky walk into the auditorium. He'd just driven in from class. I brought him onstage, introduced him, and asked, "Can you speak to these folks about growing up in an entitled culture?"

"Mom and Dad weren't perfect parents," he said, "but they did a good job on teaching us values. I remember one thing I heard a lot from them: 'You may need a lot of things, but you don't deserve anything....'"

I had to spend the next minute or so promising the laughing audience that this had not been a setup. I still don't know if they believed me.

The Right Way to Deserve

Barbi and I intentionally determined what we wanted our kids to know in this area. We had seen the bad fruit of families in which the kids believed they deserved some gift or privilege as a right. That bad fruit showed itself in a poor work ethic, self-centeredness, serious rebellion against authority, and relationship issues. We wanted our kids to know that they were safe, loved unconditionally, and would not be deprived of necessary things, and that they'd be okay. But we also wanted them to know that, while they lived under our roof, a demanding attitude would not bring them anything good. "I deserve" did not fly well with Mom and Dad.

You can't get away from the phrase "I deserve" in our entitled culture. It lurks in the fabric of our relationships and grabs the spotlight in our media and entertainment. How often you have either heard or said words like:

- "I deserve a better boyfriend/girlfriend."

- "I deserve a great job."

- "I deserve a home that is up to my standards."

- "I deserve to be treated right."

- "I deserve for people to recognize my potential."

- "I deserve to travel and see the world for a year and not lose my job."

I expressed those sentences in first person, but we often hear those sentences, or some like them, in second person too, as well-meaning friends try to assure us that we deserve something better than we have—thereby fueling our sense of entitlement without realizing it.

The problem is that we misuse the words more than we use them correctly. Most of the time when we say "I deserve," we're referring to something we desire or even need—but that's not what the words truly mean. To say "I deserve" means that you have a right to something and can therefore demand it. It communicates something much stronger than a desire or a need. In fact, this right to demand makes sense only in two contexts:

As an earned right. When you perform to a satisfactory standard in your work, you deserve appropriate compensation. You have the right to it because you have *earned* it.

When I work with a company to help it develop a fair compensation package for its employees, we talk about this. Employees who work hard and achieve performance goals deserve every cent of their paycheck and every aspect of their benefits. The company literally owes them that: "Do not muzzle an ox while it is treading out the grain" (Deuteronomy 25:4). This is a previously negotiated transaction, a binding agreement. In this context, the statement, "I deserve my benefits," is both right and good.

In the same way, an entrepreneur who creates a product that costs her a dollar and who then sells it for two dollars deserves to be paid by any customer who buys it. She has invested time, resources, and money in bringing that product to market. She has earned it.

As a contractual right to some good thing. This happens when some legal entity confers a right on a person. The Constitution of the United States, for example, provides certain rights to its citizens, such as the rights to free speech, choice of religion, and protection against unreasonable searches and seizures. U.S. citizens aren't required to put any effort or energy into securing these rights. Earlier generations won these rights and wove them into the fabric of our government, which now guarantees them. The founding fathers wanted citizens to have certain rights that would free them to have meaningful lives.

In biblical times, Roman citizens also had rights. As a citizen, Paul appealed to one of these rights: "But if the charges brought against me by these Jews are not true, no one has the right to hand me over to them. I appeal to Caesar!" (Acts 25:11). The apostle did not act in an entitled or self-centered way when he made his appeal. As a Roman citizen, he had the right to demand this kind of treatment. *Contractual rights such as these are life-giving and normal.* You deserve the contractual rights that have been gifted to you.

The Wrong Way to Deserve

The phrase "I deserve" becomes a problem when it merely expresses a need or a desire. Used in that way, it encourages an entitled attitude. As I told my kids, "Need, yes. Deserve, not so much." Things get confused and break down when we fail to make this distinction. Consider a few examples:

- "I deserve a great job." We all want a great job, but no one has an earned or contractual right to a great career. We have to train, explore, start at the bottom, take risks, fail, and work hard to get a great job. And even then, it's not guaranteed.

- "I deserve a great marriage." Everyone who walks down the aisle wants a great marriage; this is one of our deepest desires in life. But no one has promised us a great marriage.

- "I deserve to be treated well by my spouse." No one should be treated poorly. And if your mate is abusing you in some way, you should take steps to get help and set boundaries. But receiving good treatment is a need, not a right.

Deciding what we actually *deserve* has theological implications. We don't deserve God's love and grace, although he extends them to us because we need them. To the contrary, we deserve his wrath, because our sinful nature offends his righteousness: "We were by nature deserving of wrath" (Ephesians 2:3). If anyone should understand why it might not be a great idea to focus only on what we deserve, it is those who believe in Christ.

While the entitlement mantra tells us, *I deserve to be provided with a good life,* the Hard Way mantra declares, *I am responsible for creating a good life.*

This chapter will show why the Hard Way is clearly the right way for all of us.

Why "I Am Responsible" Works Better than "I Deserve"

A continual focus on "I deserve" can cause significant problems for anyone. Those who cling to an "I deserve" mentality may go through all of life feeling frustrated, unsuccessful, blaming, and empty. "I am responsible," by contrast, will free you to get where you need to go.

While "I Deserve" Weakens, "I Am Responsible" Empowers

"I deserve" directs us to some external person or power to provide something we need. "I deserve to be happy," for example, focuses on somebody else to make us happy. The problem is that when I focus on someone other than myself, I grow less powerful and more dependent. I give power to others, making it much less likely that I'll have the power to get my life together. "I am responsible to do what it takes to make me feel happy," however, puts power back in my own hands, so that I can channel that power to the only thing I can control: my behaviors.

"I am responsible" calls us to action. It drives us to go after our dreams and desires, to solve problems and to make the world—at least our part of the world—a better place. It is movement-oriented. By contrast, "I deserve" thinking leads to a passive victim mentality. People shut down and refuse to make choices. They wait for someone else to make things better for them.

I have seen many people make themselves miserable by taking the position that since someone treated them poorly in a relationship, they can say, "I deserve a better situation next time." I'm not talking here about those terrible cases where someone gets abused and violated, or about those situations where the government, the church, and we as individuals should reach out to those truly in need. Those situations do require restitution and outside help. Those are the cases in which someone has clearly and simply not treated others in a humane way.

A friend of mine went through a painful divorce to free herself from a husband who was, simply put, a bad person. He yelled at her in public—I witnessed one such incident, and it was awful. He controlled their finances, and he spent money on whatever he wanted. There were many other problems stemming from his attitudes and behaviors. After the divorce, she adopted the "I deserve a better man for what I went through last time" attitude. Not "I want" or "I will look for" or "I won't make that mistake again," but "I deserve"—do you hear the difference? I felt bad for her, because although I understood the hurt and need underneath, I knew that it would lead to problems in her dating life.

Sure enough, men quickly picked up on her demand that they be 180 degrees opposite of the ex. They heard about his abusive ways (probably much more than they wanted to). She made them feel as though it was their job to repair the damage. And on top of it all, she remained blind for a long time to her *own* contributions to her failed marriage. She never analyzed how she had picked such an unsuitable marriage partner in the first place, what she had done wrong in the relationship, and how she too often did a poor job of handling problems. She couldn't even look at these personal faults; so of course, they didn't get better.

After years of struggle, she was finally able to change her attitude to, "I need to take responsibility to find the right guy." And once she made that change, she began to see how she had often tried to rescue immature guys instead of seeking an adult male. Once her own attitudes became healthy, "right guys" began showing up. Her people picker was no longer pooped, as it were. She became warmer, more vulnerable, and more attractive to healthy guys.

While "I Deserve" Alienates People in Relationships, "I Am Responsible" Brings Them Together

"I deserve" is a statement of transaction. It means that someone owes me. It establishes a performance standard.

But relationships are never transactional in nature. They are about love, vulnerability, and connection from the heart. A transactional element flung into a personal relationship causes havoc. It can literally end the connection of love.

Suppose a husband who earns more than his wife says to her, "I have provided a home for us all of these years. I deserve support and attention from you when I come home. So give it to me." This statement throws his wife under the law. He is saying, in effect, "Love me because you are supposed to love me. In fact, you owe it to me." If anything can dishearten the outflow of love, it is this. She feels a multitude of emotions, none of them positive: obligation, guilt, fear, hopelessness, unworthiness, and anger. Under those conditions, how can she give him what he demands? Her heart has moved far away from him. She can and may comply on the outside and say nice things, but both of them will know that she doesn't feel them.

Suppose the husband says instead, "I get tired and worn out from my job. I need your support and attention when I come home. But I know you can't read my mind, so it's my job to let you know what I need. All I need is a few minutes of visiting with you when I get home. Would you do that? It will really help me." He has just shifted from law to grace. He really does have a need, but this new stance triggers her own sense of nurturance, care, and concern. Isn't that a far better way?

We can't demand love. It must be given freely.

While "I Deserve" Works against Freedom of Choice, "I Am Responsible" Supports Freedom

"I deserve a college education paid for by my parents." Besides the fact that this statement is untrue in any legal sense, such a stance also judges anyone who says no. If the parents decide that their financial responsibilities to pay for education end with their child's eighteenth birthday, then they are bad people and deserve wrath from their son or daughter. They can't say no and still be good. They're in an impossible double bind.

Think about the previous example regarding the demanding husband. If his wife says she is too wrapped up with the kids or her job to give him more time, she is de facto a bad wife in his mind. She is not free to say no and still be a good person.

And yet God never judges our freedom to choose. He encourages it, for he knows that the only way he will get a real relationship with us, from the heart, *is if we are free to walk away from him.* That is the interplay of love and freedom. *If you are not free to be unloving, then you are never free to be truly loving.* Anything else is impossible. God values our freedom enough for Christ to die for it: "It is for freedom that Christ has set us free. Stand firm, then, and do not let yourselves be burdened again by a yoke of slavery" (Galatians 5:1).

On a psychological level, this demand often reveals a serious control issue. A person makes such a demand because he is deeply afraid of rejection, of being turned down. So he demands it and judges the other person in an attempt to control the outcome. It almost always backfires.

So what's the solution? I believe it is to give up trying to control others' freedom (which is really impossible, anyway). Instead, be humble and vulnerable with expressing your needs. You'll stand a much better chance of having those needs actually met.

While "I Deserve" Is a Demand, "I Am Responsible" Conveys Need and Vulnerability

"I deserve" can sound entitled and arrogant, even when the person saying it doesn't mean it that way. People feel the demand anyway, and they often feel that they are expected to fix matters for the one expressing the need.

"I am responsible to get my own need met," by contrast, is a vulnerable statement. It focuses on what I don't possess that is important to me; it does not place a demand on others. My needs are *my* problem and no one else's. "I am responsible for my needs" is received well by others. People feel more like spending time with, supporting, listening to, and helping those who take this stance.

At a recent party, a friend brought a woman over to me and said, "I'd like to introduce you to a good friend. She's in a marriage crisis. Can you talk to her?"

The woman quickly said, "I feel horrible about even asking. You're not on the clock, and you're having fun here. So it's fine if you don't have time. I'm just honestly in a bad place right now."

Immediately I felt compassion for her situation, which I soon learned was indeed terrible. I wanted to help her because she was so vulnerable. I felt no pressure of guilt, no obligation, no "should." I talked to her for about twenty minutes, and we came up with some workable solutions.

All of us have needs in life, and it is much better for us to express them as just that—as needs, not as demands. For example:

- We need God's love and guidance—we can't demand it.

- We need others who care deeply about us, without conditions—we can't expect them to.

- We need choices and freedom—and we can't demand that other people provide them for us.

- We need finances, resources, a plan for moving ahead, and a way to express our talents—but it's our job, no one else's, to get them.

While "I Deserve" Conveys Special Privilege, "I Am Responsible" Conveys "I'll Get in the Back of the Line, Like Everyone Else"

"I deserve" communicates a "better than" spirit to others, and frankly, it does not work with healthy people. "My child deserves to play the lead in the school play," says the entitlement-based parent. Every teacher knows the damage that will come to the child in a situation like that. My wife has worked as a public elementary school teacher for her entire career, and she has seen how other parents and kids alike both react against such an attitude. When people hear it, they think, *Who do you think you are?*

We all may be unique in God's eyes, but we don't deserve a better position than anyone else because of it.

While "I Deserve" Negates Gratitude, "I Am Responsible" Encourages It

Individuals in a transactional relationship have no sense of thankfulness. There is merely a required behavior, a payment for the behavior, and that is that.

Our family has been committed to a variety of ministries and charities over the years. But recently one of my sons, Benny, a college student, found that just a few blocks from his campus were hundreds of homeless people living on the street. Their tragic lives broke his heart. We had planned to drive to his university to attend a football game the next week, and Benny said, "I want us to leave for the game early. We need to first drive to where these people are and give them food, water, blankets, and socks."

As a family, we agreed. We bought the items and put them in the trunk of the car. Benny directed us to the streets where the homeless individuals lived. We pulled over, opened the trunk, and started pulling out supplies. Within a few seconds, people came

149

from nowhere to take what they needed. Within a few minutes, all of our items had vanished.

We all felt struck by the level of gratitude we saw from these unfortunate people. Over and over again, they thanked us, shook hands with us, and hugged us. They showed no sense of entitlement or being owed. They simply were in great need. They took responsibility for those needs by coming to us humbly and without demand, receiving from us some small, simple items, and expressing their gratitude. I don't know, and I can't judge, how much of their sufferings and their station in life were caused by difficult circumstances rather than some attitude inside themselves or some unwise action they took. I am simply pointing out that we can learn from the gratitude of those who do not have.

Grateful people are prone to be happier people. Gratitude and entitlement cannot coexist in the same brain.

The Better Way

How can you change your thinking, feeling, speaking, and acting so that you do life in a way that actually works, without an attitude of entitlement? Consider these practical suggestions.

Know that needs and desires are good and are built into being human. If you want a successful life, you have to start off with desire and need. That's not selfish; that's just living in reality. Needs are how we survive, how we get resourced, and how we get prepared and equipped for making our mark in life. Desire is the emotional experience that helps point us to what we need.

Don't overreact to the entitlement culture by trying to banish all your needs and desires. They keep you alive and engaged and provide a way to connect with God himself: "Take delight in the LORD, and he will give you the desires of your heart" (Psalm 37:4).

Let me clarify: The Hard Way is *not* the Drudgery Way. Don't become discouraged, thinking that you must commit to a life of unending toil. Most people loved the idea of a book about the Hard Way as a cure for an entitlement mentality. They said, "Yes, that's right, facing up to the hard things in life is a good way to life." But a few of my friends disagreed. One of them, a business owner and a hard worker, said, "You *can't* write a book like that! I hate the idea! I'm already hard on myself and perfectionistic. I choose hard things every day. I think about your book and say, *More of this? Are you joking?*"

God designed us both to face great challenges and to enjoy life. We *should* have fun, get creative, innovate, dream, recreate, and enjoy our hobbies. And we should rest. Here is what the Preacher of Ecclesiastes wrote:

> So I commend the enjoyment of life, because there is nothing better for a person under the sun than to eat and drink and be glad. Then joy will accompany them in their toil all the days of the life God has given them under the sun. (Ecclesiastes 8:15)

No conflict exists between the two. In fact, the enjoyment part fuels and energizes the challenge part. Hard Way living should include as much joy and happiness as it does hard work.

In fact, some of my more driven executives might find out that *their* Hard Way is to learn to chill out and be useless for a while! In the stillness and quiet, they would have to deal with their feelings of guilt, overcommitment, and codependency. Trust me: To a perfectionist, that is *true* Hard Way living.

Do what you can do for yourself. If you're in a bad relationship, don't allow yourself to think, *I deserve for her to respect me.* Think instead, *This isn't working. I'm responsible to stop this madness by having a hard talk and setting some limits, or maybe by seeing a counselor.* When you see yourself as the primary agent of change rather than a person whose life is "on hold" until someone does right by you, you will take action.

As a corporate consultant, I have a habit that usually comes out at the end of the consulting day, during the executive summary session with the CEO. We review the agenda and what happened, and then we assign his or her action points and my action points. We don't end the meeting until we both have our homework. *Then* problems get solved and growth develops.

Take responsibility to ask for what you can't do for yourself. You aren't self-sufficient and you aren't bulletproof. You have needs you can't meet by yourself. To get the life you need (not the life you deserve, right?), you will need to ask people for their time, attention, understanding, support, acceptance, advice, and resources.

Live a life of abundance and giving. The world isn't a perfect place, but God still owns the cattle on a thousand hills (Psalm 50:10). When you feel (or even actually are) deprived, you tend to go into "demand and deserve" thinking. Realize that even in terrible circumstances, God loves you and will help you. He has a way ahead that is good for you and for others.

I often think about what it's like to say grace over a meal with my family or friends. Grace is the simple and humble act of thanking God for what he provides for us tangibly in our food, and intangibly in what the food symbolizes: his love, provision, and care. When I'm in the experience, all I feel is gratitude for his goodness, and there is no room for entitlement. This is how we are to be, every day, as God's people — and as growing people.

Skills

1. **Where have you most often seen the misuse of "I deserve" thinking?** In the culture? In a family? A relationship? Listen for the term in everyday conversations.

It will amaze you how often it gets said. Look deeper and discover the entitlement messages underneath that mentality.

2. **List five things you need and desire in life** and write a paragraph for each, beginning with, "I am responsible to get this need met by ..." Then get creative and come up with ideas, habits, people, and resources that will help you get these needs met.

3. **Consider five things you are responsible to do**— not for yourself, but for others. We are responsible not just for our own welfare; we were created to love and serve others as well. Be specific: a charity you believe in, a child who needs more of your time, a relationship you need to reconcile, or a service you want to perform. True happiness is impossible without fulfilling our responsibilities to serve others.

CHAPTER 9

DO THE HARD THINGS FIRST

YOU HAVE NEVER RECEIVED a winner's trophy before playing in the championship game. You have never been offered a promotion before you excelled in your job. Your parents never instructed you to make sure you ate your dessert first and not worry about the vegetables, since they would take care of themselves.

Why did none of these things happen? Because that's not how successful lives work. It makes no sense to earn trophies before you win games, get a promotion before you perform well, or eat sweets before you consume your dinner. An attitude of entitlement, though, tells us that it can and should be this way: "You can have it all. Do what is easy and comfortable first, and you'll be rewarded with a lot of amazing things."

It's a lie.

The entitlement disease's insistence that you leave the hard stuff till later (or never) results in disaster. Let's find out why.

The Next Hard Thing

Let's say you asked me to coach you in how to find your dream career. You are forty-two years old and a pleasant person, and while your current position has paid the bills, it's not exciting, it is not *you*, you have no passion for it. You want something that engages your strengths and skills, means something to you, and still provides for you and your family. This is a common scenario and an important one.

We'll begin our search for this new career track through a process of discovering your strengths, looking at the opportunities out there, and evaluating what has worked for you and what has not. With every single client I coach through this lengthy and challenging process, we will get to one particular place. That place might be that your time is taken up with work or family issues. Or that you aren't as passionate about this career-search process as when you started—the honeymoon is over. Or that you have other responsibilities—such as a friend who needs a lot of your time to help him through a divorce—that are taking your energy. That place is an important stage in your growth process. It can stall you, divert you, or derail you.

When we come to that place, I know that you're about to find what I call your Next Hard Thing (NHT). Your NHT is the choice you need to make that will get you past the difficulty. I call it hard because it almost always is. It might be simple, it might be clear, but it won't be easy. Most of the time, you'll say, "I've been here before." And yes, you have. But this time you need to do something about it—something challenging that will help you finally resolve it.

Identifying your NHT is a large part of the win. Once you know you need to say no to someone, or eliminate something good to make room for something great, or confront another person, you're almost there. But to move beyond that, there are attitudes that you must deal with to keep you moving. The entitlement mantra concerning your NHT says: *The next hard thing is too difficult, so I'll just do something else now.*

Most people succeed not by waiting, but by making a difficult choice. The better path is the Hard Way mantra, which says: *Today I will choose to do something that helps resolve my obstacle, and I'll feel better.*

The NHT can take many different forms. Maybe you'll find yours in the next few examples.

Carving Out Structured, Committed Calendar Time

A major NHT is simply sitting down with a calendar and committing sixty days' worth of time for what you want to see happen. It seems simple, doesn't it? And it actually is. But simple doesn't always mean easy.

And here's the most common reason this NHT isn't easy: *It is much harder to delete calendar items than it is to add them.* We are hoarders by nature, especially of things that seem good and positive. We're usually okay with adding items, but not so good at removing them.

Suppose you want to get your research going for that new career-search project we talked about. You're motivated, ready to go. It will probably take you about four hours a week for a couple of months before you start to see some measurable results. That sounds like a commitment, yes? Doable, but still a commitment.

Then you go to your calendar to find that time. What do you see?

- Kids' sporting events
- A job (or two) that feels all-consuming
- Church involvement
- Social activities
- An elderly parent to care for
- School engagements for the kids
- Working out
- Doctor visits

Many people don't get any further. Their mind feels overwhelmed, and the NHT never gets done. *Oh, well, I'll get to it when the dust settles,* you think. Wrong answer—that's just not how life works. The dust will settle only when *you* turn to dust.

Going against the Flow of Life

Your NHT might be a choice to get out of your comfort zone, a harder proposition than you might think. It's great to dream big dreams and have glorious visions, but a stable and "okay" life with few big hassles is a strong magnet. It tugs and tugs, saying, "Keep it chill. Take life as it comes. Don't be anal-retentive . . . like your parents."

This is the NHT of inertia. Inertia is a powerful force because it takes little energy to remain as you are, and you can still be reasonably happy that way. But putting energy into *not* being like your friends, and *not* hanging out, and doing something that matters, require a lot more of you.

Going against Other's Expectations for You

A key NHT for you might be having to let someone down who has a different future in mind for you than you do for yourself. You don't want them to feel bad; you want them to feel proud of you. But this is a trap.

A friend of mine in his twenties told me recently that he fears he will end up like his dad. And what's wrong with his dad? "He's a really nice guy and a great father," he replied. "But he never did what he wanted to do in his career, and now he's in his sixties and he doesn't have a lot of options."

I asked him to explain.

"My dad wanted to be in the architecture business. He was good at it, and he loved the creative process of putting structures together. But his dad, my grandfather, told him he needed something more stable, like being an accountant. So that's what he

160

did—and he never liked it. Plus, he wasn't especially good at it. I don't want to end up like that."

My friend's dad never went against his own father, and now he's living a sad story. Fortunately, my friend will not make that mistake. He's already seen that path, and he feels determined not to follow it. He is already making moves, even at an early stage of life, to find out what he needs to do to follow his dreams.

The late Howard Hendricks used to say, "You are able to do many things. But be sure you find the one thing you must do."

You may not have a dad to disappoint. Instead, maybe you have a spouse, someone you're dating, or another person who is important to you. God made all of us relational beings, and people should and do matter to us. But the prospect of a tough conversation with someone important—someone who may disapprove of your dream—can be a challenging NHT.

Starting at the Bottom

Especially in a work environment, you may need to begin on a lower rung than you'd like. Who doesn't want the corner office? It's humbling to work in the mail room. Entitlement becomes especially powerful in the workplace. It makes you think, *I don't deserve this. Is my boss really that much better than me?* or *This is just too embarrassing. I think I'm better off playing the lottery.* And so your NHT stops the entire process.

I had to tell a friend that his son was unhireable at anything but an entry-level position until he developed a work ethic and gained some experience. My friend felt upset by the news, but he supported my recommendation. He helped his son find something basic. The young man wasn't happy about it, and his friends called him foolish. But he found other friends, and after a year, he was on his way to management.

Crafting Your Own Next Hard Thing

I've just given you a sampling of the most common NHTs. You may face something else. Maybe you've been avoiding a difficult conversation. Maybe you haven't yet resigned from a committee that does good work, but that takes too much time away from your dream. Or maybe you need to start saving money for a project that matters to you. Or you have to tell someone that you lack the time to have lunch with them every week to mentor them. Fill in the blank.

Here are a few questions to help you identify your own NHT:

- What is the pattern that gets you stuck? Stand back from the details and look at the big themes of your life and activities. It might be kid problems, money issues, or boredom.

- What might you be afraid of? Fear can paralyze you. Maybe you're afraid of letting someone down or making them angry, or maybe you fear failure.

- What do you do with your time when you're avoiding the issue? Take a look at your "busy" behaviors: too much time online, doing Facebook or Fantasy Football, or obsessively checking email. Learn to see these as self-medications that are keeping you from your desire to move forward

- *How would I feel after I did something difficult and it worked?* You would feel hope, energy, and self-respect. Keep that image of yourself in mind to help you remember that Next Hard Things are worth it.

Pushing Past Your NHT

NHTs are true obstacles. But they're not insurmountable, and you can see some dramatically swift gains if you take up the principles that follow. If you have rammed your head against your current NHT time after time after time and have still not defeated it (or if you've *avoided* it time after time instead), then most likely you have let discouragement win. Time passes, and you become habituated to the same old same old. So as you try the techniques below, you may have a bit of concrete to break through. But it will be worth it.

Think and Talk about What It Will Do for You

Entitlement thinking resists the idea that something difficult will pay off. Hard Way thinking is the opposite; in fact, it's based on that very idea. You gird up your loins to tackle a behavior or a conversation that will bring you closer to something you desire. So think about it, talk about it, let yourself feel it. Any time a company wants to launch a new direction or product, it spends time and resources casting a vision. It doesn't simply tell its employees, "Here is the new plan." Corporate executives know that the plan will be unfamiliar, and people need to buy into the vision in order to accept it and persevere with it. People truly perish without a vision (Proverbs 29:18 KJV).

This is why people put photos of slimmer clothes on their refrigerators when they want to lose weight and why they visit open houses on Sundays even though they know they can't afford the down payment for another year or two. There has to be an image in mind, a vision, for what you want.

Don't Sugarcoat the Negative

Even if you're loaded up with vision, you need to face the truth that your NHT will involve difficulty and struggle. That's why the "H" is in the middle. The worst thing you can do to yourself is to think, *It won't be that bad—I may even enjoy it.* That doesn't work, because if you have that expectation when you hit the obstacle, you will also hit disappointment, a huge energy killer. The disappointment comes from the gap between your expectation and reality. You thought it would be a 4 out of 10 on the difficulty scale, and in reality it was a 7. That may bring your progress to a complete stop.

Instead, face reality. Don't sugarcoat what's going to happen and what it may feel like. If you've prepared yourself for what's coming, then you'll actually feel hope and energy when you encounter it. This is the kind of hope and energy that athletes experience in the locker room when the coach tells them that the next half of the game will take everything they have inside. We were born to push through things that require effort; it's in our DNA and in our essence from the beginning. We were destined to "subdue and rule" the earth (Genesis 1:28). The word for "subdue" implies imposing *order on chaos.* No matter how scary your NHT is, overcoming it requires bringing something that helps your steps be ordered to get out of some unproductive chaos and onto a path of achievement.

In the middle of a difficult divorce, a friend of mine heard something unexpected but extremely helpful from her therapist. "This process of growth will sometimes be painful and confusing," the therapist said. "You may feel like you're hitting bottom. But if you stick with this and are honest with yourself, you'll be okay and your life will be much better."

Not much sugarcoating there. But my friend said that,

ironically, the therapist's words encouraged her because she trusted and believed him. She felt that he had given her a reliable vision of the future. She could trust that vision. And after the dark times, she did get emotionally stronger, healthier, and happier.

Realize That There Is an End to the NHT

Your NHT is a temporary thing, not an eternity. In fact, it is a beginning thing, a starting thing, a breaking-out-of-inertia thing. It won't last forever.

Tell yourself, *The sooner I do this hard thing, the sooner I get my life where I want it.* The way our minds work, the more we avoid the NHT, the longer it seems it will take. It increases and expands in time. Remember that a tough phone call won't last forever. People need to get off and eat dinner at some point.

I have found it helpful to deliberately limit the amount of time you devote to the NHT. There's nothing wrong with deciding, "I'll make some calls about job interviews for an hour, then I'll go shoot hoops for ten minutes." Or "I'll call the guy to tell him our one date didn't work, and I'll talk to him on the phone for no more than fifteen minutes." My experience is that, especially in NHTs that are conversations, we hand control of our schedule to the person with whom we're speaking. It's a guilt mechanism that says, "I'll stay on the phone with you until you either feel better, or agree with my decision, or at least feel heard." That doesn't do anyone any good. Be kind and set a reasonable limit on tough calls.

Own Your Strength

An NHT has a force to it, a power to make you feel small, helpless, and weak. The longer you put it off, the larger it becomes and the smaller you become. It helps to remember that you are an adult. Adults do hard stuff all the time. They get up and go to work, they care about others when they don't feel like it, they obey God when it feels counterintuitive. Realize your own strength as a grown-up.

I have found four good ways to own your strength. Each of them will help you get moving into your NHT.

Recall your history. You have done tough things before. Bring them to mind. Think about when you asked out that dream girl in high school, when you confronted someone who was being controlling or judgmental, when you joined the gym and felt better about yourself. God gives us memory banks meant to encourage us that we have done good things, and we are capable of doing them again.

Ask God to strengthen you. All through the Bible, God encourages us to be confident in our success when we follow his paths. Read over a passage like Isaiah 41:10: "I will strengthen you and help you; I will uphold you with my righteous right hand." Go over it several times and imagine God standing behind you, supporting you in the NHT. As a good friend of mine says, "He hasn't fallen off his throne," even in regard to your NHT.

Ask a friend for his input. This is a smart thing to do, not a dumb thing. It takes five minutes. I have done it. I have coached executives to do it. Call someone you trust and say, "I am facing a mountain. Do you think I am capable of this?" It matters so much to hear the other person say, "Sure. I know you, I know what you're capable of—and I believe in you." The core of encouragement is someone believing in you when you no longer believe in yourself.

Say the words. Self-talk, or simply stating to yourself realities you need to hear, can be helpful. Research backs this up. For example, saying, "I can work out tomorrow, and afterward I'll feel better," assists your brain in girding for action and positivity.

When you listen to yourself, you hear an adult and have confidence in that adult.

Take a Step

Your NHT is about some specific behavior, and it may be behavior you have been avoiding: a phone call, setting a boundary with a friend, a conversation, cancelling a subscription to a magazine you don't need, turning off Facebook after thirty minutes. Behavior is measurable. It is not fuzzy. It is just behavior.

And behavior always begins with a step. Even a little step. It might be something that takes you just ten minutes today. That's okay. A step begins the process and puts you in a better place.

I knew I needed to work on this book today, but I was having a hard time finding the right words, as writers often do. When my wife came home and asked how it was going, I felt embarrassed but told her the truth: "I wrote five words." She said, "Great! Five more than you had before. What's next?" She had a different perspective, and hers was the right one.

Sometimes I tell a coaching client who feels overwhelmed and is therefore avoiding something to break down her NHT into substeps, tinier pieces that don't feel so daunting, like my five words. Suppose, for example, it's a phone call you need to make to tell someone you can't meet with him as often as he wants, but you can meet with him bimonthly instead of weekly.

If you're a people pleaser, your mind rushes toward how disappointed and devastated the other individual will feel. Feeling like that, you could end up postponing the phone call forever. So instead, simply calendar it: "Call Laura Thursday at 2 p.m." or "Talk to Laura at our next lunch about changing our frequency of meetings." Just calendarizing yourself gets you halfway there. Substeps work.

Accept That Hard Things Mean Making Mistakes

The perfectionist's nightmare is waiting until you do it "right." There are thousands of blank canvases where a drawing should be, an empty file folder on the cloud where a book should be, and great jobs getting taken by others because you wanted to wait until things were perfect. The first few times we do anything is generally when we make the most mistakes, whether it be a tough conversation, redoing the calendar in new ways, or disappointing someone's expectations for you. *But take that step.*

My wife and I took a trip to spend some time at the ocean, and as we walked on the beach, we saw a young boy skimboarding. He wasn't very good. He fell off the board a lot, and his board got stuck in the sand. I felt bad for him—until I realized that he didn't care. His expression wasn't discouraged, but determined.

We walked past him on our way down the beach. On our way back thirty minutes later, he was skimming much better. I heard him yell to his dad, "I'm a lot better now!" He'd started poorly, like 99 percent of us do, unless we're specially gifted. But he got better.

Within twenty-four hours of reading this chapter, do a messy step in your NHT. Maybe you'll do a bad job in the conversation—the person you called might even hang up on you. You know what? The world won't end. The perfectionist in you will start getting healthier. Take an imperfect step.

Your NHT is a lot like that stopped-up drain in your sink. It was such a pain. But when you poured in the Drano and used the plunger, the gunk broke up and you got movement. The water began to flow.

Aren't you tired of not getting past the NHT and moving on to the next step after? Break up the gunk and do the NHT.

There will be others (and lots of them!), but the first one is always the hardest. We're talking about establishing a new habit—the habit of fearlessly engaging in your NHT. It is a generalizable habit that will transfer from work to personal life to relationships and back.

Here's a silly example: When I'm at the ocean, I hate my first run into the waves. I dread the cold water; it shocks my system. But years ago, I would enter the water using the "thousand razor cuts" method: going in one slow step at a time, then gathering your courage before taking the next slow step. That felt much, much more agonizing to me. Not even close. So since then I've opted for plunging all the way into the cold surf as soon as possible. This has worked for me. I more quickly adapt to the cold, it feels refreshing, and the day is good.

Remember when I said that this habit is generalizable? I recently had to have a confrontational conversation with a client whom I liked a lot. He had a disconnected attitude with his key direct reports, which was hurting his company. He simply wouldn't listen to their legitimate concerns. I had put off the conversation for a month or so, thinking he would get better. But things were quickly deteriorating in the company culture.

During our regular phone call, as we went over our normal agenda, I knew the time had come to confront his attitude problem. When I detected a jumping-off place in the conversation, I remember thinking, *It's time to dive into the surf.* I said, "I need to talk to you about a problem that needs resolution, and it's about your own attitude." And away we went. It didn't end up being that bad. He was open to change.

Just plunge in.

Skills

1. **Identify your own NHT.** It may be in your professional life; it may be in your personal life. Write down the specific behavior you need to do.

2. **Write down what it has cost you to avoid the NHT:** Time? Money? Opportunity? Peace of mind? Freedom? Energy? Seeing the cost will help you get started. You *don't* want it to keep happening.

3. **Tell three friends that within one week you want to take that specific step.** Ask them to text you, give you support calls, and hold you accountable for that one-week window.

CHAPTER 10

KEEP INCONVENIENT COMMITMENTS

SOME OF THE NICEST PEOPLE in the world are also total flakes. They can be caring, well-intentioned, and thoughtful. Yet at the same time, they can be undependable and unreliable. I have several friends who are in this category, and truthfully, I really enjoy spending time with them. I just would not invest money with them.☺

Think for a moment about how you relate to the not-so-reliable people in your life. When you plan for several of you to go out to dinner, there's always the person about whom you say, "Well, she says she'll be there, but don't count on her. Something usually comes up at the last minute." So you tend to do a work-around with that person, because, though she is undependable, she is also likeable and fun to be with.

From time to time over the years, I have hired contractors to do home improvements, anything from carpets to cabinets. The usual process is that two or three contractors submit competitive bids for the work, and we select one. When I first started doing this, I was a price shopper. I went for the cheapest deal.

I soon realized the error of my ways. Without fail, "cheap" meant "doesn't show up."

The contractor would show up at first and dive in, which would make me happy, because my deal appeared both cheap and good. Then would come a call that he couldn't come to the house because a worker got sick, or materials didn't arrive on time. Then there would be no shows: no call, no email, no nothing. Then we would call and have arguments and reschedule our own lives around a new appointment. It felt frustrating and irritating, and if you count your own time as money, more expensive.

I eventually learned to choose instead the professionals who had great references, even if they didn't give me the cheapest bids. That solved most of our problems. Sure, I took an immediate financial hit, but they would show up when they said they would, get the work done as advertised, and stay the course. In home improvement matters, you truly get what you pay for.

Our culture of entitlement is both anti-commitment and pro-avoidance; or, to put it in another way, pro-let-it-go. Entitlement's mantra is: *If a commitment is too hard, let it go. People will understand.* The Hard Way's mantra, by contrast, is*: Do what you say you will do, the way you say you will do it, when you say you will do it.* Even if it's difficult, it is your word. The Bible affirms the individual "who keeps an oath even when it hurts, and does not change their mind" (Psalm 15:4). That "hurt" can take many forms:

- Sticking with a price that you promised even if your costs went up since you made the bid

- Getting out of bed to have breakfast with a friend even if you went to sleep really late the night before

- Continuing your giving percentage to church and service organizations even when you are in a downturn financially

- Being on time to a meeting even if you have to leave another setting early

- Not needing someone else to remind you to do errands or chores—just taking the initiative to do them yourself

- Calling someone who has been struggling and to whom you have said, "I'll call you and check in on how you're doing"

Recently, my family and I were invited to have dinner with another family, new friends we really wanted to get to know. It was a spontaneous thing, an invitation in the afternoon for dinner that evening. Earlier, however, we had made plans to spend the evening with old friends. This get-together could not easily be rescheduled, and, more importantly, we would have had to cancel at the last minute. We had a brief family meeting about it that took about twenty seconds. We had made a promise to our longtime friends, and that was that. We felt sad that we couldn't visit with our new friends, but there's a right way to do things.

Have you ever been on the other end of this—as in being the "old friend" who gets cancelled? It's not a pleasant experience, and it hurts to have someone cancel on you because something better came along.

The Little Thing Is a Big Deal

It may sound like no big deal, but making and keeping inconvenient commitments is a truly important matter, at all levels of life. Commitments are promises, and promises hold the world together. Civilization could not survive long without enough people keeping promises—even hard-to-keep, inconvenient commitments. Think how critical commitments are in our world:

- *Contracts*. Business is built on contracts, which are documents consisting of promises. Company A promises to deliver a product to Company B by a certain time, for X amount of dollars. If both parties get it done right, everyone is happy. If A or B reneges, the contract gets voided, and then expensive and messy legal problems may result.

- *Marriage vows*. At their wedding ceremony, the bride and bridegroom make promises to each other to be faithful and supportive in sickness and in health, for richer or for poorer, in good times and bad times. This is one of the

175

deepest commitments a person can make, for our nature is to bail when things become difficult. I have worked with many couples who have weathered very tough stuff, such as betrayal, indifference, or abuse, and yet they have made it past that and now have a close and intimate union. One thing that kept them together during their hard times was remembering and being true to the covenant of marriage, even when they felt hopeless, and even when they had no positive feelings left for the other person. The covenant held things together while they worked on their growth and healing. And eventually the hope and the loving feelings returned.

- *The laws of the governing bodies.* The world has laws, which are legal rules designed to maintain some amount of order and justice. Law is a commitment that provides protection and safety to the people governed by that law. When we live without law, we have anarchy and chaos, and innocent people get hurt.

Gaining Trust from Others

One of the most important reasons to keep hard promises is because *it is the only way for others to learn to trust you.* Business and success research have both supported what the Bible says about the importance of trustworthiness: "The LORD detests lying lips, but he delights in people who are trustworthy" (Proverbs 12:22). We naturally gravitate to trustworthy persons.

I have a close friend, Bob Whiton, who might be the most trustworthy person I know. I have known him for many years, and I can't think of one time he said he would do something that he didn't do how and when he said he would. Our families have

176

grown close, and we have even done business together, so we have had lots of interactions of many kinds.

This is a man who is early to lunch appointments and gets me email info I need on time. He has stayed with our family when the kids got sick. He is solid through and through.

Here is how much I trust Bob: When I'm at a doctor's office as a new patient, and the forms I fill out ask for an emergency contact besides my wife, I put his name and cell number down. I've done this for many years. Think about what that means. If something catastrophic happens, he gets the call. And I know that he will drop what he is doing, drive to the hospital, find my family, or do whatever is needed, no matter how difficult or inconvenient. He might even jeopardize himself.

Here's another important aspect of trustworthiness: *Bob and I see each other only once or twice a year.* We are no longer in business together and our families live in different locations. But my conviction that he is the go-to guy has not changed one bit.

Who is your Bob? Do you have one? Think about it, because you need one. Just as importantly, are *you* a Bob? I am not, at least not at Bob's level. I am not as Olympian in my trustworthiness as I'd like to be. But I'm working on it, because I have a good model, and that model has borne great fruit in my life in security, safety, and confidence.

The Two Kinds of Trust

There are two major kinds of trust that exist in our relationships with others, and great things happen when your behavior becomes trustworthy in both of those types of trust. As you read the descriptions that follow, ask yourself which of the two takes more effort for you. That's the one you should work on first. I'll suggest skills at the end of the chapter to help you.

Functional Trust

This type of trust is equated with reliability or dependability. You go to great lengths not to let people down in some task, behavior, or assignment, because you know it's important. Here are some examples:

- You get reports in to your team at work before they're due, to avoid traffic jams; people aren't "on hold" for you.

- You arrive at lunches and coffees a few minutes early. One of my professors told me, "It's almost impossible to be right on time. So your options are to be either a bit early or a bit late." Be the first one there.

- When you tell someone you'll be at a function, don't cancel at the last minute because a better option came up. Show up.

- When you borrow money from a friend, don't make him have to nag you to get it back. Be the one who writes the check on time, before being asked about it.

I have seen individuals in the companies I consult with who have enormous talent and personality but have lacked functional trustworthiness. And they have lost everything because of it. Business and organizations absolutely require this trait.

Relational Trust

This is the trust that comes from being a safe person when someone gets vulnerable with you. A relationally trustworthy person can hear her friends be open and honest about what I call the Big Five:

- *Mistakes*: "I made our lunch all about me when you needed support."

- *Struggles*: "I don't feel like I am being a good parent to Amelia."

- *Weaknesses*: "I have a hard time saying no to others."

- *Needs*: "I need you to listen to me vent about my marriage."

- *A vulnerable emotion*: "I feel overwhelmed." (Or anxious, sad, or embarrassed.)

The Big Five are difficult to bring up to just anyone, though we all feel all of them at one time or another. They embarrass us; we feel like damaged goods. We don't want to be high maintenance, and we don't want to feel judged.

So think about what someone is telling you about your relationship when they sit down and open up about one of the Big Five. They are telling you something important. They are saying, "I trust you with me."

What are you supposed to do with this level of trust if someone shows it to you? If you listen to entitlement, you'll do the following:

- *Make it about yourself*: "You think that's bad? I flunked every class in third grade!"

- *Give premature advice*: "I know your dad is really ill, but you need to be strong and move on."

- *Keep it light*: "Besides that, Mrs. Lincoln, how was the play?"

- *Keep score*: *Hmmm. She admitted a mistake in the sales meeting. I can use that later.*

These "entitlement" responses are easy. Anyone can do them. But going deep is not easy. It's inconvenient. It brings us face-to-face with our own wounds, mistakes, and struggles. It's messy. But it is also what makes possible both success and great relationships.

Consider the key behaviors of a relationally trustworthy person, the kind you want to be:

- *Move toward their struggle, not away*: "I had no idea you were so upset. Tell me more."

- *Go out of your way*: "Sure, I can come over. It sounds urgent."

- *Let your friends have their feelings, giving advice only after you've earned it by listening*: "I'm sorry to hear about your fight with your husband. You must have felt awful." Then, when you have earned the right to give advice, you might say, "You might want to let him know, without being vengeful, that this behavior has to stop and you guys are going to see a counselor."

We all need to be both functionally and relationally trustworthy in relationships, marriage, business, parenting, friendship, dating, and church. Life just works better that way. So put the energy in. If you are involved in some level of leadership in an organization, a similar reference for the two kinds of trust can be found in the *New York Times* bestseller *The Five Dysfunctions of a Team* by Patrick Lencioni,[9] one of the world's leading business consultants and thought leaders. He explains his view of these types of trust from a team-building perspective. I find his ideas helpful.

Get the Obstacles Out of the Way

Of all the entitlement issues I deal with in people, the problem of promise-breaking seems to generate the most excuses and rationalizations. I think this is because it's a behavioral pattern that's apparent and easily observed. People impacted by an entitled person's constant breaking of commitments (inconvenient or otherwise) will often confront the entitled person about it. But instead of changing, the entitled person will tend to excuse it. Here are some examples of the reasons people have problems with keeping commitments, and of the reasons they excuse themselves for doing so.

Making Commitments You Don't Have the Resources to Keep

When you care about people, you want them to be happy. Or if you tend toward being a people pleaser, you might be driven by a fear of letting others down or disappointing them. Either one of these motives can easily cause you to drift into writing a check with your mouth that your actions can't cash. So you scramble to keep everyone happy, but you don't have the bandwidth to do a great job or be on time, and either it all falls apart or it's mediocre at best. The result is that people end up being unhappy and disappointed, just the opposite of the effect you wanted, but even so, brought about by your own inability to keep your promises.

I worked with an executive who had this very problem. He wanted to be seen as a can-do guy, but he kept letting people down and frustrating them because he overcommitted to projects, decisions, and meetings. He didn't know how to fix that. Finally, I told him, "You need two simple tools to help you, and they should fix a lot of this overcommitment problem.

181

"The first is what I call the 'five-second delay.' When people ask you for lunch, or a meeting, or a commitment of some kind, you must give their request five seconds before you reply. You can't say yes or no until you have waited at least five seconds, so that you can actually think about whether you can do it. You need to engage your brain and check your calendar before you commit.

"At first, it will be an uncomfortable practice for you. You are such a people pleaser that I have seen you say yes to requests for your time even before people had finished asking! But no one will be bothered by this. Just look like you're thinking or say 'hmmm' so it won't feel awkward for the person who's making the request."

"I'm not crazy about it," he said, "but okay. What's the second one?"

"The second tool is the words 'I don't know.' You don't have to say yes or no to someone asking for your time or attention. You are free to say you don't know, especially if you don't know. Executives often feel a demand to have an immediate answer, and that actually makes their direct reports more dependent. The words 'I don't know' convey, first, that you are honest, second, that when you do have an answer, it will be one that you have carefully thought about, and third, that you trust that they can handle ambiguity and not require a black-and-white answer. And if you are a rock star, when they ask, 'So when will you know?' you can say, 'I don't know. But I'll let you know as soon as I know.'"

My client found both of these two tools hard and unnatural, at least at first. They tore at his desire to keep people happy. He didn't like frustrating them. But after a few experiences, it got better, and good things started happening. His people liked that when he said yes, he actually meant it. And they started trusting him, because his behavior cashed the checks that his mouth wrote. As Solomon wrote, "It is better not to make a vow than to make one and not fulfill it" (Ecclesiastes 5:5).

If you tend to stay around the get-together or the party too late and therefore are not as ready for the next day as you'd like to be, you will also tend to be without the resources of sleep and energy. Here is something I learned that works. As a social animal, I tend toward staying late with friends, so I had to come up with a better tactic. I now leave when about half the people have left. I don't feel a compulsion to tell every person good-bye, as I used to. I tell the hosts good-bye and smile and walk out without a big production. No one has ever told me they felt I had abandoned them, because I hadn't. And while part of me would like to stay on, I find, using this approach, that I feel satisfied with the fun and relational time I had, and I get to bed on time. A small tactic, maybe, but it helps.

Not Wanting to Be Perceived As Rigid

No one wants to be perceived as OCD or a stickler about rules like being on time and paying debts. It looks nerdy, anxious, and weak. The timekeeper on a team, on a board, or in a Bible study often gets tarred with the brush of caring more about punctuality than about relationships. They get labeled as the "parent" or the "classroom monitor." Who wants that? As a result, people don't make a big deal out of keeping promises. It seems better to them to be a bit more relaxed.

There's certainly nothing wrong with being relaxed; we all need that. The thinking behind this obstacle, however, is what is called a zero-sum game. A zero-sum game is the attitude that when one thing increases, the other must decrease. If you increase time for goofing off, for example, you have to decrease time for working out. That's just the physics of it. But being highly relational, even relaxed, and keeping promises and commitments don't conflict with each other. In fact, they coexist very well.

A close friend of mine pulls this off beautifully. A successful, friendly, and funny guy, he navigates through life effortlessly. He's a people person. I've been to many social and business events with him, and he connects, hangs out, listens, and is interesting. No one would see him as rigid, and everyone wants to hang around with him.

And I have never been to a meeting with him for which he did not show up early and prepared. He is ready to go and gets things done. His secret is that *he plans way ahead in private, so that he seems relaxed in public.* He spends a significant amount of his office time scheduling, allowing for travel (and even possible traffic problems), so that he never feels rushed.

This is the answer to the "I don't want to be seen as rigid" obstacle. *Don't* be rigid. Make promises, but when you do, plan the time and energy you need to fulfill them.

Thinking That People Will Understand

Some people don't work hard at keeping commitments because they believe that they get graded on a curve. This belief system says:

- I'm a good person and I have good intentions.

- I try my best.

- People will see that I am trying.

- I give people a break and they should do the same with me.

This is understandable. We should be understanding and recognize that people have good hearts and are trying hard. But at the heart of this belief system lies a much darker and unhealthy assumption: *I am entitled to be judged on my intentions and not my actions.* This quickly becomes a demand that no one hold me accountable for the fruit of my behaviors. It's entitlement speaking once again, and it's bad for everyone.

One morning while away on business, I texted my wife and asked her to bring my sunglasses from home to an event we would attend after my flight landed. "Sure," she said. Then one of my sons texted me: "You texted Mom and asked her for a favor and didn't mention that it's her birthday." Feeling horrible, I thanked my son for the heads up and went to damage control. I had forgotten her special day. I had overcommitted my time, and I confess I was thinking more about talks and flights and sunglasses than about her birthday.

I called, told her how sorry I felt, offered no excuses, and she kindly forgave me. But how do you suppose that conversation might have gone had I said, "You know how hard I work for us! You're an understanding person, and you know about my tight schedule. I'm sure you are okay with this." It would not have been pretty.

Get rid of the demand that you be graded on a curve. Instead, when you consider not following through on some commitment, remind yourself: *If they feel bugged with me about this, it's not their fault. I let them down, and I have to deal with the results of my choice.* This reality-based reminder will help you focus and follow through.

The Bottom Line: Empathic Love

Ultimately, the determination to keep inconvenient commitments comes down to empathic love for others. If you care about people, you care about how your behavior affects them. When you are reliable and responsive, their jobs go better, they feel better, and their lives go better. When you let them down by failing to keep your commitments, *even when you don't intend to,* people you care about have their lives disrupted in some way.

My failure to acknowledge my wife's birthday made her sad. This wasn't about me fulfilling an obligation so I could check it off the "good husband" list. It went far deeper than that, and I felt heartsick because I had made her feel sad. That is empathic love. And it is what Jesus taught in his Golden Rule: "In everything, do to others what you would have them do to you, for this sums up the Law and the Prophets" (Matthew 7:12). Treat others the way you want to be treated.

This is not a guilt message, and I hope you won't take it that way. Rather, it's a reminder about impact. We all impact the people we love, for better or worse. If we do not impact them, we don't matter to them, nor they to us. This is just reality. So think about how your behavior affects your family, friends, and work relationships. Those thoughts will help you make and keep the right commitments.

Skills

1. **Think about how much you care for two people in your personal life and two with whom you work**. Because you care for them, you want them to have good lives and to be happy. Then write down how you think they must feel when you let them down. They might be discouraged, or feel alone, or simply be frustrated. You don't want to negatively impact those you care about, and writing down this information will keep you mindful of how important others are to you.

2. **Write down three areas in which you feel that you continually let yourself and others down.** You might include being late, or changing plans abruptly, or being unavailable to someone when they need you. Don't guilt or shame yourself about it—that's not the purpose of

the exercise. Just pay attention to it and figure out why it happens. It probably happens due to one of the three obstacles listed on pages 181 to 184. Begin dealing with this tendency every week.

3. **Ask a safe friend to help you increase your success in this area.** If you are late 60 percent of the time, in the next thirty days you can easily get it down to 20 percent simply by staying in touch with a person who will help you remain aware of it.

CHAPTER 11

RESPECT THE FUTURE

MY SON RICKY is in his early twenties and has entered the workforce. I was having dinner with him in the city where he lives and works now and told him about this book. I asked Ricky how his generation experiences entitlement issues.

He put his fork down and said, "One thing we—people my age—are in trouble with is the YOLO mentality: 'You Only Live Once.' We ignore the reality of tomorrow and get stuck in today."

This tendency to have an unbalanced relationship with time itself afflicts not only millennials but the culture of entitlement in general. Good things don't tend to happen in one's life when you live only for today. To state the obvious, time is important—it's critical, in fact—and we need to understand how to relate to it.

How does our understanding of past, present, and future, and our approach to each, relate to success in life?

- *The past*: What has happened before and is now part of the hard drive in your brain. If our life has been normal, "the past" is filled with meaningful and cherished memories that make life richer and with lessons we have learned to become skilled, wise, and successful.

- *The present*: What is happening right now. Right now, today, you are making choices and decisions that matter.

- *The future*: What is to come. Though only God knows the future, we know that it's in consideration of the future that we make decisions about the life we dream of and the life we don't want, and we analyze what it takes to achieve the first and avoid the second.

When we pay attention to all three time periods, life goes well for us. The lessons of the past and an anticipation of the future guide our present's direction and tell us where we should put our energy and effort.

YOLO, however, focuses on only one of these, the experience of *the now*. It says, "Since life is fleeting, you may die tomorrow and the future is unsure. So have *today* the experiences that matter." What are the implications of that attitude?

- Why save for a future that may never come?

- Working extra on the weekends for a long-term career dream could be futile, so have fun instead.

- If you're not enjoying your job, just quit—right now, impulsively, with no thought or planning or a new job lined up—and follow your instincts.

- That relationship seems hopeless, so instead of seeking answers, getting help, and trying solutions over time, get out while you can and go be happy.

No one would argue with the importance of living in the present. God designed creation so that we live and breathe in the present. When we lose current experience, we are only half alive. I have worked with many executives who, in the second half of their lives, had deep regrets that they had driven hard on their career goals only to miss being emotionally or physically present at their kids' upbringing, their marriages, and the beauty and excitement of life. If they could do it all over again, they say, they would live more in the here and now.

In fact, it would be fair to say that many of these executives have children who have adopted YOLO because the kids saw the difficulties and emptiness of their parents' lives and turned away from it. One young man told me, "My dad made a lot of money and had a little life. I want a big life, and if I have to give up a lot of money to get it, that's an easy call."

But here is the problem, and it's a huge one: *YOLO alone will ultimately fail you.* Focusing only on the present is just as dysfunctional as focusing only on the future. The adult child and the parent both lose out. I don't want that to happen to you, so I've designed this chapter to help you respect the reality, the power, and the potential of the future. And you don't have to lose today to do it!

Entitlement and the Future

The entitlement mantra about the future is: *Ignore the future and focus on today.* But the Hard Way mantra is: *Respect the future and let it guide today's experience.* And why should we respect the future? Here are four reasons:

One Day You Will Experience Your Future

Your future is not "out there." Very soon, it won't be called the future; it will be called *Now.* And you'll experience it, feel it, touch it, and taste it, for better or worse.

The future certainly will arrive—and as much as possible, we want to think about the things that we will experience before they overtake us.

Think of it this way. Small children don't have the skills to truly understand the impact of the future. Their neurology and emotions are all about today and now. One of the roles of a good parent is to get children to consider the future. "If you bonk your little brother on the head, you'll be sitting in a time-out chair in the kitchen." The pleasure of dominating a sibling feels less inviting when a future of no freedom seems likely. This is why parents need to follow up on their promises about consequences for certain behavior. If your promises amount to empty threats, maybe because you feel tired, your child will learn that the future is not to be respected. *All I have to do*, he thinks, *is get used to a nagging parent*. But a competent parent imposes the consequence consistently so that the child actually experiences the future consequence as a present-day reality, and therefore respects it.

Adults too need to respect the future. We aren't bulletproof, any more than children are. In business, CEOs sign contracts in the present and need to honor them in the future even if circumstances change. If you are a young adult, your toned body will become more difficult to maintain as you age. As Rick Warren says, "I used to have a six pack, but then it turned into a keg."[10]

Bill Hybels says that "we tend not to drift into better behaviors."[11] He means that over time, our energy, our bodies, and our focus lose steam. That's just the nature of things. If you are over the age of thirty-five, look in the mirror after you shower. This truth will be evident. Because we do not tend to drift into better behaviors, we must constantly put resources northward to help combat this southward erosion of life. The older you get, the more time and effort you must devote to moving against the flow. Tomorrow is coming like a train, and you will experience either what it is like to jump on board and have a great ride or what it feels like to be left standing on the tracks with nowhere to go.

A Groundhog Day *Life Doesn't Work*

Let's look a little deeper into your present, the life you live today. You may be struggling with major difficulties. Or you may be in the okay range, where things aren't ideal but they're good enough. Or you may be enjoying a fantastic life.

No one wants a life of major struggle to continue forever. That would feel miserable and hopeless. And few people are content with just "okay" forever. That's just a halfway satisfying life; sooner or later, those with such a life wake up and think, *I settled. And I paid a big price for it.*

I don't even know anyone with a *fantastic* life who wants everything to stay the way it is *forever.* Even people with a great life still want growth, improvement, and change. And the most self-satisfied and complacent among us—such as the Pharisee in one of Jesus' parables, the man who said, "God, I thank you that I am not like other people" (Luke 18:11)—aren't seen in a positive light.

A life that does not change and improve is like the movie *Groundhog Day*, in which Bill Murray's character repeats his life over and over again until he becomes completely miserable. Even his successes become meaningless.

And that's why you must respect, consider, and act on your future. Because if you don't, your best possible case is *Groundhog Day,* where you, your relationships, your career, and your life stay stuck in a repetitive pattern. Same thoughts, habits, patterns, struggles, and activities. When you don't think in the present about the future, you get trapped in an endless loop.

My kids have friends who didn't leave for college after high school, though they could have. Nor did they find something meaningful to do in town. The result is that they have become objects of pity to their friends. Often they continue to hang out with much younger high school kids, reliving their "glory days," because that's where they got stuck emotionally.

Some of my own friends live in *Groundhog Day.* They don't spend energy on the future, such as where they will vacation next year or where they hope their kids will go to college. I find it hard to spend a great deal of time with them, because I see so much potential for them to develop their talents, find more passion, take risks, and experience transformational lives. Instead, I feel sadness, discouragement, and frustration for them.

Some of these friends have escaped the loop by starting to hang around people who draw their attention to the importance of their future (perhaps men and women in a great church or from a small group or a movement). And some have broken out of that wasteful pattern because they encountered great loss, such as a child on drugs or a divorce. But too many of them continue to play Bill Murray.

While Your Past Is a Closed Door, Your Future Is an Open One

Respect the future because it is not over and done, as is your past. It is yet to be decided, and there are so many possibilities.

On the one hand, you can't undo the past. You can't change your mistakes, wins, and losses. That door is closed. On the other hand, you can learn from your past, and it can be redeemed in your growth and healing. But there is no "do over."

Not so with the future.

I'm a big believer in blue-sky thinking. With my business clients, I do a lot of "let's start with the ideal" brainstorming about the company, its potential, and what might be possible. I'll set up a whiteboard and say, "It's a blank slate; fill in your future." Inevitably, creative, innovative, exciting ideas fill up the space. We are built to think about and get energy from the hope that comes from a bright future.

When this catalytic energy occurs, regardless of whether we're talking about your company or your personal life, it's bound to change your present behavior. You will be more strategic about how you spend your time, money, and energy. You will be more disciplined in how you choose your relationships. You will be driven and fueled by a hope for a much better future. When you respect the future, you dramatically increase your chances of attaining a better one.

The Magic of Compounding Today Creates a Great Future

Financial managers use the term "the magic of compounding" to describe a great benefit that accrues when you respect the future. When people save and invest well early in life, the money saved and earned increases at a high rate over time. When people begin to save later in life, they can't take as much advantage of the magic of compounding. Time is on your side when you save from an early age.

The magic of compounding is one variety of the concept of sowing and reaping. The better and earlier you invest your time, talents, and treasures, the better the rest of your life will be. Healthy marriages, families, careers, spiritual lives, and bodies are all the result of reaping from earlier "sowing." Early is always better.

A friend of mine who reviewed this manuscript told me about a client of hers whose motto was "one day at a time." This client wanted to be free of anxiety and dread over the future and wanted to keep her life simple. So she never saved, never watched her diet, and didn't study up on how to create and maintain great relationships. She literally lived one day at a time. Now in her later years, she is having great difficulty. Retirement will be a problem for her. She has diabetes from her poor eating habits and chaotic lifestyle. And she enjoys no stable relationships.

"One day at a time" is actually a helpful statement when used in context. I use it when I work with people in Alcoholics Anonymous who feel overwhelmed by their many life struggles.

But you must balance "one day at a time" with being respectful of the future and guiding your daily decisions by how they will impact you tomorrow.

The Talk of the Two You's

Because we live in the present, we need reminders that the future exists and that it will be just as real as the present, sooner than we expect. Sometimes those reminders come in the form of graphs, charts, and progress spreadsheets. Sometimes they take the shape of the people you ask to support you on some structured and regular level, to keep you working toward the future. And sometimes your reminder can be you yourself. I use and exercise what I call "The Talk of the Two You's."

Because it provides hope and feels good, it is easy to fantasize an unrealistic future that has no relation to reality. For example, you imagine that you will lose fifty pounds in a month. Or that with a 2.5 GPA, you'll get into Harvard. Or that you'll move to L.A. and become a millionaire in two years. But in fact, this mentality is just as disrespectful to the future as ignoring it, and it bears the same fruit. Both strategies wind up with *Groundhog Day*. Or worse.

In fact, MRI brain studies have shown that thinking about the future activates different areas of the brain than thinking about the past. And when we don't connect our present realities to our future self, the "future self seems like a stranger."[12] So fanciful thinking becomes hopeful thinking, which then, as it gets deferred time and time again, "makes the heart sick" (Proverbs 13:12). The result is discouragement and passivity, not an outcome you want to experience.

I created a scenario to help my executives deal with these two issues. They needed help in reminding themselves to respect the future and to look at it realistically. I have found it highly effective. It is rooted in imagination.

Imagine a conversation between the present you (the one reading this book right now) and the future you, ten years from now. Suppose you had an opportunity to hear what the future you would want you to know. Wouldn't that be helpful? What would your future you say to your present you? Consider a few examples:

- "I wish you would have kept the big picture of your vision and goals in mind more. You drifted from thing to thing and from day to day, and now it's going to be a lot more work to get some dreams accomplished."

- "I'm glad you decided to become more focused on what your life is really about and finished your degree so that you could get a job that fits your talents. It has made a great difference in the last ten years."

- "I wish you had put energy into the relationships that really mattered. You let controlling, critical, or selfish people take up way too much of your time, energy, and love. It would have worked out so much better if you had set limits on these relationships so that you could instead invest in supportive and positive people. Your life would be different today."

- "I remember when you said goodbye to those toxic relationships and started hanging out with people who wouldn't drag you down but instead supported you. It wasn't easy and you felt bad and guilty ... for a while. Then it paid off in dating and marriage and in your career."

- "I wish you had done 90 percent less Facebook and TV. You became passive and sedentary, and you lost some of that great mind and creative energy you had."

- "It was a great move when you started working out regularly, cut your social media and TV down to a few minutes a day, and started helping out at the food bank. The world, and you, were better for it in the last ten years."

- "I wish you had had a better balance of work and play. Feeling good and having good times took over, and your career suffered."

- "When you started meeting with people to help with your career, got coaching, and took those skills-training weekends, it improved your future greatly. You're still fun, and your hard work has paid off."

I regularly do this exercise for myself. I actually look in the mirror and say what comes to mind, as I imagine the "me from ten years in the future" giving the present me advice and perspective. This exercise has been highly effective for me in respecting my own future and staying connected to reality. I don't always enjoy it, except for the parts where I say, "Hey, you paid attention to what was important, and that worked out well, so keep it up." It's often hard, as when I hear the future me telling the present me things I don't want to hear. But doing things the Hard Way helps minimize my own regrets, which is important to me. As I mentioned in chapter 5 on motivation, you want as few regrets as possible. Regret is one of the most painful emotions we can feel.

Deal Successfully with "Future Feelings"

If you really focus on the future, which leads to productive action in the present, feelings may arise that you'll need to deal with so that they don't trip you up.

The positive feeling about the future is *anticipation*. I describe it as a "visioning emotion" that helps us do hard things for a future goal. Anticipation is what athletes feel when they get close to some noteworthy achievement. It's what an executive feels when she sets a killer strategic plan in motion and watches it unfold. You will feel anticipation when you begin your vision and plan (before reality hits), and when you feel confident that your plan will actually work. When you feel anticipation, embrace it, talk about it, journal it. You need the fuel that comes from anticipation. Don't let it slide into obsessive *Okay, back to work, what's the next step* thinking. That robs you of the benefits of anticipation.

The number one feeling that results from thinking about the future, however, is not as positive: anxiety. When people fear what is coming, when they feel insecure, when they feel dread, doom, or a catastrophe in the making, they feel anxious. Anxiety is a sense of heightened tension. It is a type of fear. It is a feeling that something bad that you cannot control is going to overtake you. It is an alert that tells you that you want to avoid a bad or sad tomorrow.

We need a certain amount of anxiety. It keeps us getting up in the morning so that we won't lose our job, keeps us biting our lip rather than verbalizing what we really want to say when the guy on the freeway cuts us off, and helps us set limits with our kids when they push us beyond reason. Those things are called *adaptive anxiety*, something that gives us just enough of an edge to keep some guardrails on our behavior. It's adaptive anxiety that provides that adrenalin surge that causes us to say no to a present temptation that would have diverted our time and productivity, taking us out of the game for the future.

But there is another level of anxiety called *overwhelming anxiety*. Overwhelming anxiety paralyzes us and keeps us frozen in fear. It creates the "fight or flight" syndrome that pushes us into behaviors that don't help us.

I once worked with an executive who felt such great anxiety about meeting with his board that he could hardly speak to them coherently. We had to work on reducing his anxiety from the overwhelming level to the adaptive level. After that, he presented himself well.

Here is the point: When you start focusing on respecting the future, expect the anxiety. People who try to avoid anxiety at all costs *tend to become anxious about feeling anxious.* It's like when someone says, "Don't think about a purple elephant." Our minds tend to direct themselves toward what is prohibited. Don't fight it, or it will get worse.

Remember: If you think about tomorrow in the right way, you will structure today in a manner that will yield something to look forward to in the future. Tomorrow can be your friend, not something that disappoints you: " 'For I know the plans I have for you,' declares the LORD, 'plans to prosper you and not to harm you, plans to give you hope and a future' " (Jeremiah 29:11).

The future truly is your friend. And thinking about it rightly will help you in the present with focused behavior, good self-control, direction, and ultimately fulfillment. Pay attention to it. A today with tomorrow in mind will place YOLO in the proper priority every time.

Skills

1. **Get rid of the attitude that keeps you bound to YOLO thinking.** Face the negative fruit in your life that staying stuck in the present has brought you (and will continue to bring you). Consider what you're likely to reap through YOLO sowing. Henry Cloud's chapter "Play the Movie" in his book *9 Things You Simply Must Do*[13] can help you greatly in this process.

2. **Have the talk between your present self and your future self—the Talk of the Two You's**. It will show you perspectives, insights, and emotions you didn't think you had. Write down what you learned so that you can remember it and review it later.

3. **Structure intentional time to think about your future.** Within the next week, spend an hour alone thinking on, and writing down, your dreams and goals. What do you really want that you have refused to let yourself consider? Even if it seems unreachable, write it down. Better to have several blue-sky goals and check off the unrealistic ones than not to have enough. It can actually be a pleasant and positive experience.

4. **Ask three people to help you direct your behavior with the future in mind**. When you slip into *This is what I need and feel today, and that's all that matters* thinking, this team of three can remind you that you are better than that and need a better future than such a mentality will provide.

CHAPTER 12

THE PEOPLE FACTOR:
FUEL OR FAILURE

WHILE TRAINING one of my leadership teams about the kinds of relationships that high-performing leaders should have, I asked the group, "When you are discouraged, out of gas, or just down on yourself, where do you go to remedy the situation?"

The answers ranged from, "I try to break the situation down and analyze the causes, to get a good solution," to "I get out of the office and take a walk to clear my head," to "I work out; it helps with my endorphins," to "I talk to my spouse when I get home."

Several hours later, I asked another question: "So what do you do when you know one of your key employees is discouraged, out of gas, or just down on themselves?" They had quick answers: "I'd drop by their office," and "I'd be there for them," and "that's part of my job and mission."

I pointed out the disconnect between their two sets of answers. "You aren't walking your talk," I said. "You guys would so be there for others you care about. But why would you disqualify yourself from receiving the same help that you would give others?" The question led to a conversation that resulted in the executives beginning to do better in getting their own relational needs met as well.

The problem we highlighted that day revealed a symptom of a disease that all individuals, not just leaders, experience: the tendency to default toward self-sufficiency.

Self-sufficiency, as described in chapter 3 on "God's Framework for the Right Way of Life," is an attitude of reaching only to the inside of yourself for what you need, instead of reaching outside for relational support. It tears people down and increases their entitlement. This chapter will help you to help your entitled person to move toward the right, health-producing relationships.

In healing an entitlement culture, relationship is a make-or-break factor. It truly matters. Whether we carry the entitlement disease or not, our lives and our destinies are marked by the company we keep. Relationships make a huge difference. How we connect with others doesn't change the Hard Way to an Easy Way. It simply makes the Hard Way work as it should.

We are a relationally driven species. Relationship is one of the core sources of all we need to make life work. Relationships are not just an accelerant to our success—they are essential to our very survival. Throughout the stages of life, whom we choose to let inside and whom we choose to keep out will impact both what we want and need out of life and how successful we are in achieving it.

People fuel your energy, positivity, resilience, and creativity. They can help you to become someone you never dreamed you could be. They can influence your capacity to achieve your potential and to find health, success, and meaning in life. This influence can be positive—or negative. The relational sword cuts both ways.

Entitlement drives people away—at least the healthy ones. It's hard to stay connected to an entitled person. That's why many entitled people have significant relational struggles or tend to unerringly pick the wrong people for relationships.

The Hard Way mentality understands a crucial reality: *I need people to fuel me, and I need to fuel them as well.* You will never lose your need for the good things relationships bring. And you will be happiest when you are also delivering fuel to others. That's because you and I are part of a larger task: We are involved in the growth of the body of believers. "From him the whole body, joined and held together by every supporting ligament, grows and builds itself up in love, as each part does its work" (Ephesians 4:16). We source one another and are sourced by each other. Our dependency on each other keeps us fueled and ready to engage in life.

The Unhealthy Dependency of Entitlement

Entitlement, too, creates dependency on others—but in unhealthy ways. Entitled individuals need others to keep their decisions, their sense of stability, and even their finances in working order—*but without having to disrupt their self-centeredness.* This is sometimes hard to see, since many entitled people perceive themselves as independent, free, and having no need of others. To admit otherwise would go against the grain of their grandiose self-image. It's a little like the teenager who says to his parents, "I don't need you guys for anything! I'm fine without you. And by the way, can I have my allowance?" But those who have the entitlement disease are at their core dependent people, whether or not they realize it.

Why this strong dependency? Because the entitled individual *requires help in staying away from reality.* The impact of entitlement is anti-life, at least the life God intended, which is full of love, consideration, empathy, and diligence. So *the entitled person's life principles work against God's life principles.* And since that person is blinded by his own entitlement, he's unable to see that the universe around him, having been created by God, operates according to God's life principles. He is like someone in a rowboat trying to paddle upstream in a flooding river; he can work hard at it, but he'll still fail. So unconsciously or consciously, the entitled individual seeks relationships with people who will help them to, first, avoid the unpleasant truths about their lives, and second, make their dysfunctional lives less likely to fail completely.

If you have read any of my books with Henry Cloud on bound-aries,[14] you'll remember that when you don't set good boundaries with people, you run the risk of protecting those people from the experiences they need to have, to help them own their behavior. That's why one of the first questions I ask the leader when I work with a company or a family is, "How are you enabling this atti-tude?" In other words, let's see whether you might unknowingly be part of the problem because you're rescuing the entitled person from the impact of their negative behavior.

Here are the three types of relationships entitled people tend to be dependent on, and some examples of changes that can happen for the good. Entitled people tend to seek out people who "help" them by:

- **Avoiding reality: shying away from confronting the entitled individual for fear of conflict or of discour-aging her.** This protects entitled people from hearing how their attitude and behavior impacts others—and themselves. The entitled person gravitates toward these people because he needs them (and can count on them) to be affirming, encouraging, and positive and never to address the negative behavior. Such people *feel* safe and supportive to him, but far from being safe, they're actually keeping him from being aware of his actions. When I work with a company that has an entitlement problem, one of my first training topics is to help the leadership learn the skills and courage to create a culture of support *and candor*—not simply support.

- **Enabling: excusing her behavior because they feel bad for her or don't see her as a mature, responsible person capable of making right choices.** This protects entitled people from experiencing the natural consequences of their choices. Enablers support the entitled person financially when what she really needs is to take ownership of her money, her debts, and her lifestyle. At work, enablers excuse disrespectful behavior and a lack of responsibility either because they feel that their enabling is in fact an appropriate expression of love, or because they see the entitled person as a victim who has no choice but to be the way she is, or because they gain a sense of satisfaction from helping in that way. I worked with a family who had an out-of-control teen. The turning point came when the mom finally said, after years of enabling, "If she keeps on this way, she's going to have a bad life, or hurt herself, or hurt someone else." Having gained that perspective, the mom finally found the strength to truly help her daughter.

- **Bad modeling: living a life of entitlement themselves so that they and the entitled person who sought them out see life the same way, with neither of them seeing anything wrong with the unproductiveness or destructiveness of their behavior.** Entitled people find friends who support their denial of responsibility and their sense of specialness. They tend to see others who are not part of that lifestyle as controlling, unaccepting, and judgmental—they feel that such people "don't understand them." This includes employers, parents, spouses, and other friends. Friends who share a sense of entitlement support each other in tuning out more helpful and honest voices. One talented but entitled executive I worked with, who was coming close to losing his job, finally realized that his "supportive" friends were just keeping him tied to a troublesome lifestyle. He made space in his life for a few other friends, friends who were just as emotionally supportive but who also gave him good feed-back (the straightforward, no-holds-barred type, such as "I'm worried that if you don't change, you're going to lose your wife and your kids"). And he began changing.

My point is simple: Entitled people are like anyone else. They are, by design, relationship-seeking beings. The problem is that they tend to choose relationships with those who help them maintain their entitled perspective. That's a problem. But the good news is this: *That very need can help bring them the right ingredients of growth.* Here's how.

Relate to Them in Better Ways Yourself

First, make sure that you're not part of one of the three groups above: those who avoid confronting, those who enable, and those who model entitlement and keep the patterns going. Tell the entitled people in your life the truth about their impact, even if you are afraid they will have a negative reaction. Love them, but allow them to experience natural consequences, even if it's difficult. Live life the Hard Way yourself, and stay as far as you can from the behavior patterns and attitudes of entitlement. In other words, don't be an agent who increases entitlement. Be a relational force who helps resolve it.

One of the most powerful examples of this is not when a new relationship deals with the entitled person in better ways, but when an ongoing relationship changes the rules. I have seen parents, employers, and friends help make dramatic transformations with individuals they have been in relationship with for a long time. This is so effective because the attachment is already in place. It's as if a longtime dance partner suddenly starts making different moves. It feels disruptive and uncomfortable, but it leads one to be more open to change. The old dance patterns don't work as well anymore.

I was working with a couple in which the wife was highly entitled. She made disagreements a nightmarish experience. When her husband would express an opinion different from hers on her parenting, or their spending, or their communication, or when he would confront her about something that bothered him, she would fly into a rage. She would yell and verbally abuse him. Because her entitlement made her think that she should never be confronted or disagreed with, his differing with her offended and angered her.

Because the husband hated arguments and wanted to "keep peace" in the family, he avoided confronting her about her behavior, and he also enabled that behavior. He made excuses for her behavior, such as "She's been under a lot of stress." Not surprisingly, the problem was getting no better.

When I met with the husband, I simply told him, "You are both the number one most important problem and the number one solution for your wife." I explained to him the new, different ways in which he needed to relate to her. I said, "You matter to her. You can't fix her, but you can be with her in ways that make her entitlement less effective for her and make being responsible work better."

The first thing I had the husband begin doing was this: just walk out of the room when she began yelling at him. She expected him to just stand there and take it, trying to calm her down, because that's what he had always done. When he began saying instead, "If you don't talk respectfully, I'll leave the room"—and actually doing it—it made it less fun for her. Who wants to have a tantrum in an empty room? It disrupted and confused her, and in time, she began curbing her behavior, because it wasn't working for her any more.

The Best Ways to Relate

In addition to those three "don'ts," those three patterns of behavior to avoid, here are two helpful and healthy ways to relate to those in your life who are into the Easy Way.

- **Be truly "for" them.** Entitled people need support! Even when they drive you crazy, frustrate you, and make you feel helpless, they still require the elements of grace, care, and love. The need for the fundamentals just doesn't change. A diabetic with a bad attitude still needs his insulin, and a self-absorbed person with a broken arm still needs a splint. It's easy to write off an entitled person. But before you do, remember that we all have failed, and we all need second and even third chances: "Out of his fullness we have all received grace" (John 1:16). This will help you to have mercy and identify with the person, keeping you away from being judgmental or giving up too soon.

- **Be clear about what you need and expect from them.** Entitlement often causes people to not listen well to requirements and to others' needs and expectations. Because those things don't support their view of themselves as special and above the rules, they tend to dismiss them. Do all you can to defeat this dismissive attitude by being unmistakable in what you want from them:

  I expect you to meet your weekly work goals.

  I need for you to pay us rent while you are living with us.

  I want you to ask me how I'm doing and listen to me tell you about my day when we talk.

  I expect you to do more than is required, if you want to be promoted.

Clarity requires that you don't assume anything in your relationship with your entitled person. Better to be over-clear than to have futile conversations about "How was I to know?" You help him and yourself by being straightforward.

Support Better Relational Choices

You are not enough. No matter how important you may be to the entitled person, she needs more than the elements of health and growth that you can provide. You can't be her only lifeline and support system. You don't have all of the love, empathy, support, wisdom, or strength she needs. It is not within you. God's plan has always been about community: "Love one another" (John 13:34).

That is why the more you can help your entitled person to connect with good "one anothers," the better the outcome. When I was operating a psychiatric hospital program, one of the main factors that determined success or failure once patients were discharged was whether they returned to the old social systems that had supported their dysfunction or instead they found new and healthier relationships. I have found the same thing to be true with leaders and executives as well. The ones who begin pruning back their toxic connections and finding new and better relationships instead also performed at higher levels in their organizations. *We tend to operate at the level of health of those we surround ourselves with.* It's hard for our bodies to perform well when we're not eating the right foods or are eating too much of the wrong ones. The same is true with mental health. Here are some ways you can help:

- **Find health.** Look for friends, churches, counselors, and coaches who are full of grace and truth and who could be a resource for your entitled person. Entitled people tend to have poor judgment about who they let into their lives.

So do a bit of research. Find a healthy church in your area that has strong couples groups, personal growth groups, spiritual directors, trained pastors, Celebrate Recovery groups, and referrals to good therapists. Your company's HR department will have lots of resources to help as well. They may have specialized training in entitlement, but if they don't, just encouraging health is a big step. Find where the best relational health resources are in your area. In my opinion, offering your entitled friend or coworker this kind of help isn't being codependent or enabling. It's supporting them. It's doing something for them that they can't do well for themselves. By the way, I have become a big fan of phone and videoconference growth relationships. For both coaching and counseling, they can be effective. If I have to choose between an okay local coach and an A-list coach out of the area and only available by phone, for example, I always go for the best-quality help.

- **Be vulnerable about the "why."** Let your entitled person know that you want them to create new relationships, not to change them or fix them, but because you love them and want better for them. It's vulnerable to say that you are concerned, to say that you care. If instead you say that you want them to improve (unless this is an employer/employee relationship), it comes across as parental and one-up and will likely create resistance.

- **Add before you subtract.** It's tempting to tell an entitled person to drop all the "wrong" people he has in his life. You have seen how they drag him down or keep his self-centeredness strong. But don't do it. He has attachments, and attachments are powerful, even if they are not healthy ones. Much better to encourage him to connect with a few

216

people who are the right people for him; let him begin to experience a healthier and happier life as a result of those relationships. That way, he will be more likely to gradually drop the toxic elements over time, because they have been replaced.

Think about how important relationships have been in your own life. They have helped you choose the path you have chosen. They may have even helped you shed some of your own entitlement. Relationships — the right relationships — will make a great difference in the life of your entitled person.

Skills

1. **Dig deeper into your own growth relationships.** If you want to see changes in your entitled person, the most important thing you can do is to continue growing, being vulnerable, and strengthening yourself personally. Commit to spending time being authentic, transparent, and vulnerable with your own life team. Resist the tendency to put too much energy into repairing the other person. Health brings health.

2. **Seek relational help for your person from trusted and successful sources.** Fortunately, you don't have to reinvent the wheel in finding good resource people. Good HR departments, counselors, and churches have been helping provide solutions for this issue for a long time. Ask around your community. Simply saying, "I'm looking for help for someone I know who has issues with entitlement" will tell them a great deal so that they can help you.

3. **Practice your pitch.** There's always a risk that you'll come across as perfectionistic, parental, and superior to your entitled person when you suggest new relationships. Prepare: Find a safe person and role-play the conversation. Let him coach you and tell you how to come across more vulnerably but still clearly.

CHAPTER 13

SAY "I WAS WRONG"

I WAS COACHING an executive couple on their communication skills. The husband had just, for the fourth time, interrupted and corrected a story his wife was trying to tell. She had tried to be patient, but finally she became hurt and exasperated.

"Maybe I need to let *you* tell the story," she said. "I can't even finish a thought about this and I'm not having fun right now."

I stopped the process and said to the husband, "Are you aware that she's right? You've corrected the story several times, and honestly, I'm feeling pretty sorry for her right now."

He objected: "I was just trying to correct some of the factual inaccuracies in her story—you know, dates, places, people. Those things are—"

"Hold it right there," I said, interrupting on purpose. "This is a major reason you guys need coaching. Put the factual inaccuracies on the back burner. They are not important now and probably never will be."

"But I was just trying to help her—"

"With all due respect, hold it right there again," I said. "Look at your wife's face. What is she feeling?"

He looked at her. "Hurt and sad."

"Yes, hurt and sad," I said. "And pretty withdrawn, too." I turned to her: "Is that how you're feeling?"

"Yes," she said.

I turned back to him: "When you've hurt someone's feelings, the last thing you should do is explain why you did it, as if that makes it better. I mean that literally; it's the *last* thing you should do. Which means that at some point it might be helpful, but not now."

"What's the first thing?" he said, more engaged now.

"Say you were wrong."

"But I was just—"

I interrupted him again. "Seriously, don't go there. No more 'I was just' anything. If you want a real connection with your wife, do not say this."

"But—"

I sat forward in my chair so that our faces were close. "Just say you were wrong," I said. "Look at her and say you were wrong. And mean it."

I don't usually have to be this forceful, but I knew there was a lot at stake in this relationship.

He went silent. I could see the frustration growing on his face. I knew from talking to his wife, his kids, his employees—and I had now confirmed in the office—that this man had not often said those words.

Slowly he turned to his wife. She looked back at him, waiting quietly. "Honey," he said slowly, "I was wrong, I'm sorry."

She didn't do cartwheels; in fact, she pushed back a bit. "About what?" she asked.

"About that thing I do."

"What thing?" She wasn't twisting the knife. She recognized this moment as a critical juncture in their relationship and wanted clarity.

"That interrupting thing."

"You really think you did something wrong?"

"Well, I was just trying to—"

It was my turn. "Nope, stick with it."

He was really becoming frustrated.

"Maybe it will help," I added, "if she tells you how your interrupting makes her feel." I turned to her. "Can you do that?"

She said, "Like we're not a team, and I'm an idiot who can't get anything right." Her eyes moistened as she became more vulnerable.

He softened when he saw her hurt. "Honey, I had no idea you felt this way. You're my everything and my teammate, and a really competent person I respect."

His words seemed to comfort her, at least a bit.

"So now," I directed him, "answer her question."

"Yes. I really do think I did something wrong. I took control of the conversation and it was dismissive and rude. And I do it a lot with you. I'm sorry. I don't want to ever do that again."

Again, she didn't turn cartwheels. But I could see her feeling closer to him, with a tad more hope.

Long story short, he was a man of his word, and he learned the habit of letting her tell her stories in her way. But that wasn't the big *aha* for him. It was learning how difficult it was—like pulling teeth—for him to admit he was wrong. That process took us a great deal more work, using the skills and principles outlined in this chapter. Learning *that* part was much more transformational in helping him obtain the marriage, the family, and the business that he truly wanted.

The Power of Confession

What's the big deal about saying, "I was wrong"? It certainly was a big deal for my client. But his discomfort isn't nearly as important as the benefits that come from it.

I have noticed a pattern in my work with people, a sharp contrast between successful individuals and those who stay stuck in life. It's an inverse relationship: *Successful people point to their failures, while failing individuals point to their successes.* While there are certainly exceptions to the rule, the pattern is that the mega-achievers have no problem bringing up their massive screw-ups—in fact, they seem to enjoy it. I think their character is integrated, with lots of ambition, but with little shame and self-judgment. I had one high-performing leader tell me about a deal in which he'd made millions, and then he finished the story with, "And I found out later that the other side negotiated better than I did, and I could have done twice as well. But, oh well." He didn't seem embarrassed at all, nor did he speak as if he had an image to protect.

By contrast, with the second group, you can go through all sorts of contortions in a conversation with them, and it's like trying to wrestle down a greased pig to get them to admit fault. They will describe how they were cheated, or how circumstances worked against them, or how bad the timing was.

This inverse relationship is no coincidence. The successful try things, make mistakes, look their mistakes in the eye, learn, and try again at a more informed and educated level. In this way, they're likely to achieve even greater success over time. And the failures feel helpless, victimized, and unlucky. Sadly, they're doomed to repeat their pasts over again—until they learn the value of "I was wrong," followed by no buts.

When to Say, "I Was Wrong"

Life gives us multiple opportunities to practice saying, "I was wrong." For instance, you could say, "I was wrong when I . . .

- didn't finish school and decided to play harder instead."

- slacked off at work and lost my job."

- made my marriage about me and not about serving my mate."

- thought I could live like I was nineteen when I was thirty-six."

- didn't stand up for myself in a terrible relationship."
- rescued and enabled my adult kid and drained myself."

None of these are fun things to say; instead, they're all *great* things to say. These statements will get you somewhere, and you'll see why in this chapter.

Ultimately, it's about confession. Basically, the statement "I was wrong" is a kind of confession, or an agreement that something unpleasant is true. We need to confess things all the time: I must confess that I didn't answer the email soon enough. I have to confess that I overspent on the credit card. I need to confess that I haven't been the person I should be. I should confess that I robbed the bank.

(Okay, just kidding on that last one.)

You are simply saying, "Yes, I did it." It's not a pleasant or enjoyable thing to say. I say it all the time to my family, friends, and business associates, and it never feels fun. But "I was wrong" has unbelievable power to cure entitlement and to give you a launch into a great life. Let's consider the amazing benefits of "I was wrong."

You Can Fix What You Confess

And on the flip side, you can *never* fix what you *don't* confess.

If a company asks me to consult with them, the first thing I do is spend a day with the management team. I interview people, look at reports and financials, and observe how they interact in a team meeting. At the end of the day, I give them a diagnosis: "Great organization, but you need more targeted marketing," or "more seamless systems," or "a healthier culture." If they agree, they are confessing that something is wrong and needs improvement. In that case, we are on our way to making things better.

But if they say, "*My* department isn't the problem—it's the other guys," and the other guys say the same thing, we have nowhere to go and nothing we can fix.

It is the same thing in relationships. When neither side "owns their stuff," be it selfishness, withdrawal of love, control, judgmentalism, deception, or irresponsibility, the couple simply has nowhere to go and nothing they can fix. That is why, when I work with couples, I spend a lot of early time having people discover and take ownership of their own contributions to the connection problems. It's hardly ever 50–50, and sometimes it's 90–10. But I've yet to see a totally innocent partner in a relationship problem.

One of my rules is, "If you're spending more energy focused on the issues of your partner than on your own, *even if the person is an addict or a felon,* you're never going to be happy or healthy." Why not? Because until you do your own "I was wrong," you won't learn what inside of you keeps you rescuing, enabling, or putting up with bad behavior.

This is one of the main reasons it's so difficult to become a Christian. You can't just join the club and start going to church. You have to tell God, "I've sinned." In other words, "I was wrong." What a humbling statement! And yet it's a requirement for accepting Christ's sacrifice for your sins. If there is no disease of sin to confess, there is no sense or logic in receiving the antidote of forgiveness. Listen to John: "If we claim to be without sin, we deceive ourselves and the truth is not in us. If we confess our sins, he is faithful and just and will forgive us our sins and purify us from all unrighteousness" (1 John 1:8–9).

And yet look at the benefit from the spiritual side. You can fix, or God will fix, what you can confess. The problem of guilt and alienation from him gets erased forever. The central reality of life has changed.

"I was wrong" is a very, very healing sentence.

People Identify with Those Who Own Their Stuff

Think about the last argument you had with a person who would not admit fault. He or she diverted, blamed, dismissed, changed the subject, played victim, and used any number of other tactics. Didn't it feel awful? Didn't the time go by slowly? Didn't you feel helpless?

Nobody healthy wants to be around someone who can't say, "I was wrong." We all want a mutual connection that goes back and forth, with one person saying, "I screwed up an account today," and the other saying, "I was late for my kids' soccer game for the third time." When I am in these conversations, I relax and, even knowing there will be difficulty, I feel energized and connected. No pretense, no defensiveness. We're all in the same boat of being imperfect people. What a relief!

I was doing an executive summary with a CEO of a day I spent with her team. It had been a tough day, because the company was struggling and many of the problems pointed to failures in her leadership. Though she was highly relational and supportive, she often avoided tough decisions such as confronting poor performance and letting go of long-term employees whose entitlement led them to behave as though they shouldn't have to work hard.

I went over the issues with her in her office, telling her, "A great deal of the challenge is about your lack of boundaries and follow-through on decisions." I didn't know what she would say. I was so gratified when she said, "I've always known this at some level but didn't want it to be true. I'm pretty disappointed in myself, because it is true. This is my company and I will change this."

She did change it, and the company benefitted. This CEO's capacity to admit when she was wrong changed everything.

People Feel Safer

When you say, "I was wrong," after truly wronging a person in some way, you are telling them, "I am aware of how I have impacted you, and I care about that." Rather than randomly smashing plates in someone's kitchen and then saying, "Well, I was careless," you say, "Those plates were important to you, and I am really sorry about how poorly I treated them." I call this an *impact statement*.

Impact statements draw people together and make them bond and trust one another. Just like the executive husband at the beginning of this chapter, people warm up to "I was wrong and I know how I affected you."

I asked the wife in the story that opened this chapter why she warmed up to her husband after he confessed and made his impact statement. She said, "There were two things. First, I felt like if he could see it, then it was less likely that he'd do it again. But the most important part was that I could tell how bad he felt that he had hurt me. When I saw on his face how bad he felt about his impact, and I could tell it was real, I felt understood and I wanted to be close to him again." Those are the two reasons people feel safe: less likelihood of a negative reoccurrence, and seeing an empathetic response to the damage we do.

Hard, Hard, Hard

"I was wrong" is one of the hardest statements for us to make. Why does it stick in our throat? Because it does.

The entitlement mantra is: *I can't admit fault. I would look weak and ashamed.* The Hard Way mantra is: *I need to admit wrong readily, because it will set me free.* Let's identify and resolve several of the obstacles to confessing that we were wrong.

Habit. Unfortunately, our culture of entitlement has trained us to avoid taking ownership at all costs. It is a deeply engrained, universal habit. Watch *Judge Judy* or experience a child custody battle or just read the celebrity breakups in *People* magazine. It gets vicious. The finger-pointing becomes extreme. In our culture, it's normal to blame. The ratio of "it was me" to "it was not me," whether it be on TV or at a party, is a very low fraction.

Our spiritual heritage. To add to that, we are born blamers, just like Adam and Eve, our parents. It's in our DNA, from the very beginning. When we caught our kids with their hand literally in the cookie jar, they made up some of the most creative lies about it. Sometimes their excuses just made us laugh: "My brother made me." Uh, your sibling *made* you take and eat a cookie? That had to be one of my all-time favorites.

But one of the jobs of parenting is to help kids grow out of the blame game so that when bad things happen, the first thing out of their mouths isn't a reactive "not me!" but a thoughtful "Let me think what I might have contributed to this mess." Through good parenting and good example, kids can learn the habit of taking the beam out of their own eye (Matthew 7:4–5).

Self-judgment. Sometimes people don't admit fault because it goes beyond "uncomfortable." We all have an inner judge who can grow harsh and condemning. And to look at our true condition and its negative impact on others can feel unbelievably painful.

I was working with a family in which the father had made some poor financial decisions that gravely impacted the entire family and its future. He had not listened to sound advice or the appeals of his family, and he had made some unwise and highly speculative investments, using their savings and the equity of their home. It had all come crashing down.

We had a very, *very* tough meeting. The dad got quite defensive: "I did the best I could for my family! I had bad advice! You all don't support me!" But the family pressed on toward his impact on them. Finally, at one point, I saw his face change — and it was not a good change, as in remorse. "Maybe I'm no good to anyone," he declared. "Maybe I need to not be around."

I got him to a psychologist's office ASAP, and he stabilized. But it was a scary time. What was behind this man's self-harming thoughts was a harsh, internal voice of judgment that skewered him to the point of despair. He had always been a strong, silent type, hard on himself. And he had little experience with receiving grace, support, or love. When you have little grace inside, the judge runs rampant. The law truly brings wrath (Romans 4:15), and his self-wrath was horrible.

The good news is that after he had been in counseling a while and had received support from his family, he was able to admit how destructive his financial choices had been for them and how sorry and remorseful he felt for making them. He had internalized enough grace to tolerate his wrongdoing, which gave him the compassion for his family members that they needed to hear from him.

Could something like this be your obstacle to saying, "I was wrong"? Perhaps you fear that if you admit something, you will fall into a black hole of self-hatred. That does happen in rare cases, like this one. If so, surround yourself with a God and people who are full not only of truth, but grace as well (John 1:14).

Knowing and saying. Some people don't admit fault, even when they know they are wrong, because the very act of saying the words out loud to someone is so painful. They feel bad inside, but it is hard for them to bring their failures out in a relationship. They feel shame and guilt that they would prefer to avoid.

That is a unique aspect of relationships. While, left to ourselves, most of us can compartmentalize negative realities about ourselves and think about something else to avoid them, not so when we connect. When we talk to people about our failures, the emotional awareness of what we have done comes to the surface, and it becomes much harder to avoid and pretend it's not there. It's like what happens when you drop an Alka-Seltzer tablet in a glass of water. The water releases the potency of the tablet, which was inert until then. Relationships release how we really feel and what we really know about our actions. So many entitled people simply avoid admitting fault to others, intuitively knowing that they might feel some reality that will be difficult to deal with.

Our language. We use all sorts of word games to avoid saying, "I was wrong," and these games negate the value of our confession. Here are a few things never to say again, along with some healthy alternatives:

- "It wasn't my fault" vs. "I may have been at fault, I will truly think about this."

- "It wasn't that bad" vs. "It was wrong, and that's that."

- "I'm not hurting anyone but myself" vs. "I have an impact on people who matter to me."

- "They made me" vs. "They influenced me, and then I made my own choice."

- "I'm sorry you got your feelings hurt" vs. "I'm sorry I hurt you."

You're not alone! I still sometimes catch myself using these word games. But you get better the more you work on it.

It's Worth It

I have seen many success stories in people moving from entitlement to success via the Hard Way, and a great deal of it has started with saying, "I was wrong."

I have seen a board of directors forgive a CEO for making bad decisions and give him another chance.

I have seen a mom who alienated herself from her kids by constant criticism gain their affection and love.

I have seen marriages rebuilt and families healed.

And I have seen unsuccessful people who have never gotten their act together and pridefully blamed others finally break down, own their errors, gain support, and find great careers and opportunities.

It happens all the time.

"I was wrong" is not the end of things, but the door to new things. After confession comes repentance, as sure as after the doctor's diagnosis comes the prescription. But *nothing substantive happens in our lives until we humble ourselves enough to say the words* "I was wrong," whether it be about how we fail ourselves, or fail others, or fail God.

Make "I was wrong" a normal part of your vocabulary, and then watch what happens.

Skills

1. **Lean toward "overconfessing" this week.** Say, "I didn't mean to go on about myself" or "I think I came on too critical" or "I was ten minutes late and that took time out of your day." These are little things, but they will help you become aware of the benefits and power of stating when you are wrong about matters, even small ones.

2. **Read Psalm 51:17:** "My sacrifice, O God, is a broken spirit; a broken and contrite heart you, God, will not despise." This is a great passage to help you experience the power of confession and the nearness and closeness of God as a result.

3. **Write down the number one thing** that has kept you from the career, happiness, relationship, or direction you have been seeking. And it can't start with someone else's name! Start with "I have been wrong in how I have avoided hard things" or "I've been waiting on someone to give me permission to take risks" or "I have depended on my parents to bail me out of hardship." Read it. No, it isn't pleasant, but it's the best surgery. Then start taking actions so that you'll never have to say, "I was wrong" about that specific mistake again. There will be others! But you can begin to change that one this week and get on with enjoying a new life.

CHAPTER 14

FACE THE PAIN THAT GETS YOU SOMEWHERE

IT'S AS SIMPLE AS THIS: If you want to get somewhere meaningful in life, you need a relationship with pain. You must understand how to use and experience your own pain in ways that get you where you want to go.

This principle lies at the core of Hard Way success. Elite athletes understand this; so do military professionals and other high-performing groups. It may be physical pain, emotional pain, or relational pain, depending on your goal. Once you accept this principle and establish your relationship with pain, you will find yourself on your way.

Clearing the Air

Simply put, pain is *discomfort*. It is a negative experience or feeling of any stripe or category. It might look like any of the types in the following list. (These are just examples for the sake of discussion. Each of the categories has many more examples — you can probably add many on your own.).

- *Physical*: feeling sluggish and tired from being overweight
- *Emotional*: feeling overwhelmed, sad, or anxious
- *Relational*: feeling alienated and alone from someone you love
- *Career*: feeling frustrated with a lack of fulfillment in your job track
- *Financial*: suffering losses and struggles in your money management
- *Spiritual*: feeling disconnected from God and his grace

No one enjoys (let alone loves) the feeling of pain. It hurts. When you put your hand on a hot stove burner, you yell and quickly yank away your hand. You respond to that extreme discomfort as we all naturally do: We want to *get away from it!*

Let's clear the air about one thing that will help you to find success in your relationship with pain: *Life has no pain-free option.* Life has no path on which we have no negative feelings, experiences, or relationships. It doesn't exist, no matter how much we would like to find it.

I call the quest for that path the Nirvana Search. People on the Nirvana Search constantly look for ways to avoid discomfort and difficulty. They don't choose to exercise because it makes them uncomfortable. They don't take career risks because they might fail. They don't engage in difficult conversations because they would rather think positive thoughts and "not go there" with challenging people. They take shortcuts. They find it nearly impossible to do hard things for an extended time.

And they never do find Nirvana. They don't even come close.

But who can blame a person for the Nirvana Search? It would be crazy to love pain; in fact, the love of pain provides strong evidence of a psychological disorder. As you'll see in this chapter, however, while it might be crazy to love pain, *it is sane to love the results of the right kind of pain.* It makes sense to love the reaping that the right kind of pain inevitably sows in your life.

I have never met anyone who successfully pulled off the Nirvana Search. Sooner or later, we all encounter difficulty and discomfort. It is simply impossible to never hurt, never get disappointed or fail or lose, never feel frustrated. Life doesn't bow its knee to us; it's much more likely to roll over us. And we really can't medicate eternally the hurts we feel. Life is far larger than our self-medication.

In my experience, those who hold on to the search more

stubbornly than others are either three years old or drug addicts. Both groups seek pleasure and avoid pain at all costs. They dedicate a lot of life and energy to those feel-good-at-any-cost endeavors. While drug addicts need treatment to help them conquer their condition, three-year-olds need wise and loving parents to guide them into accepting that, while life can be good, they need to accept the presence of pain as a permanent part of their lives.

Entitlement attitudes resist pain. The culture of entitlement constantly presents options to avoid pain of all sorts. Entitlement offers fixes for each of the painful life categories I mentioned above:

- *Physical*: Begin one of the many instant, dramatic weight-loss fixes.

- *Emotional*: Distract yourself by eating or working so you won't have to feel the distress signal from your emotions.

- *Relational*: When a relationship gets tough, bail out and start over.

- *Career*: Don't take jobs that require working overtime and weekends.

- *Financial*: Go into credit card debt and pay it back later.

- *Spiritual*: Remind God that it's his job to make you happy and solve your problems.

Entitlement has a simple mantra for all pain: *Feel good at all costs.* Life is short, feeling good works, and you should never have to experience discomfort for any reason.

The Hard Way also has a simple mantra for pain: *Face the pain that gets you somewhere.* The two are diametrically opposed—and while the Hard Way works for you, the entitlement way always fails you in the end, just as surely as the instant weight-loss program you began won't result in lasting weight loss.

Remember the definition of the Hard Way: *The habit of doing what is best, rather than what is comfortable, to achieve a worthwhile outcome.* All of this ties together, which explains why I say you need to create a relationship with pain that works well.

Since no sane Nirvana path exists, let's look at what a helpful relationship with pain might look like. We'll start with the two types of pain.

Symptom Pain and Success Pain

The first kind of pain I call *symptom pain*, a sharp discomfort that alerts you to the reality that you need to do something new and different. Consider it a warning. The six pains listed in the beginning of this chapter are all examples of symptom pain. They say to you, "Hey, look! You have a problem, and it's time to deal with it." And if you don't deal with it, they may amp up the intensity until you *do* deal with it. C. S. Lewis calls pain God's "megaphone."[15]

You want to diminish your symptom pain as much as you can, but you can do this only by figuring out what lies underneath the symptom, its root. You must address whatever is causing the pain so that you can succeed, solve problems, and have a healthy life.

And the key to diminishing symptom pain is the second type, *success pain*.

Success pain is different from symptom pain. It is the discomfort that helps you change and grow. It is good for you. It provides answers, hope, and energy. It may be *just as uncomfortable as symptom pain*, but so what? It brings you good fruit and makes it all worthwhile.

Success pain is also the best way to diminish symptom pain. It is the tree that produces the fruit. This is so because it is the work we have to do about an underlying issue that we have been avoiding, which has led to the symptom pain in the first place. When we face the success pain, we help resolve the symptom pain.

Let's revisit the six symptom pains, and see the success pains that we need to address:

- *Physical*: feeling sluggish and tired from being overweight

  Success pain: Find a support system and a balanced nutrition/weight plan and stick to it.

- *Emotional*: feeling overwhelmed, sad, or anxious

  Success pain: Bring to your life team the loss, injury, or struggle that is driving those feelings.

- *Relational*: feeling alone and alienated from someone you love

  Success pain: Learn some healthy confrontation skills and have that difficult conversation.

- *Career*: feeling frustrated and having a lack of fulfillment in your job track

  Success pain: Get a career mentor or coach and calendar some time to work on your passion, talents, and training.

- *Financial*: suffering losses and struggles in your money management

  Success pain: Take a Dave Ramsey course, learn the skills of budgeting, and stick to the plan.

- *Spiritual*: feeling disconnected from God and his grace

  Success pain: Talk to a safe and mature pastor or spiritual director about what is going on and what steps you might take to reconnect to God.

Do you see the pattern here? All of the success pains are work, they are effort, they require energy, they are difficult, they take time. They feel painful. *And they resolve the symptom pain.*

The Bible says the same thing: "Therefore, since Christ suffered in his body, arm yourselves also with the same attitude, because whoever suffers in the body is done with sin" (1 Peter 4:1). God designed a path to help us be done with sin, in all its forms: the sins of failing, of letting yourself down, of not reaching your potential, of being locked into dysfunctional relationship patterns, of being imprisoned by bad habits and addiction, of not taking care of our bodies and our weight—in other words, missing the marks that God has for us.

God's solution is suffering—but the right kind of suffering: "Whoever suffers in the body is done with sin." That is success pain. It is uncomfortable. We feel success pain literally in our body, in the form of fatigue from our workout, feeling anxiety about that tough conversation, boredom from having to go to yet another job interview, feeling overwhelmed with emotions when we deal with our past. But it produces good fruit, and it's worth it.

We have a lemon tree in our backyard. When I look at plants, they shrivel up and die, but my wife has the ability to nurture plants. Suppose I went out to grab a lemon to make some lemonade and found the lemons dry and withered. In my disappointment, I might say, "You really need to be big and juicy. You're pretty much a failure as a lemon."

Any self-respecting lemon would say to me, "This is your problem, not mine. I'm just the fruit. Nothing will improve until you fix the tree." And that would be true. If we added better fertilizer, water, and sunlight, odds are the lemons would be much better. No amount of confronting the lemons will change a thing.

Jesus used the metaphor of fruit to help us understand growth and the lack of growth: "Every good tree bears good fruit, but a bad tree bears bad fruit. A good tree cannot bear bad fruit, and a bad tree cannot bear good fruit" (Matthew 7:17–18). God's structure is to deal with the tree.

"Facing" My Pain

I recently had to "face" my own symptom pain to get this message. My face literally was the symptom.

I woke up one morning to work with two clients who were coming to my home for a scheduled engagement. My face felt numb, but I thought it was because I had slept in a funny position. I stood in front of the bathroom mirror and rubbed my face to get the blood going.

Nothing happened. My face remained numb.

In fact, the left side of my face refused to move. I couldn't move the left half of my mouth, my cheeks, my eyebrows, or my forehead. When I tried to talk, my words came out slurred. I thought I had suffered a stroke, so I tried all the left side/right side movements of my body, and everything else worked fine. So I ruled out a stroke, but I had no idea what was going on.

When my clients came to the door, I told them what had happened. Fortunately, one was a health professional who took a look at me and said, "Get in the car. We're going to the ER." On the way, he called another health professional friend of ours and the two of them both thought it looked as if I had Bell's palsy.

I had never heard of it. They described it as a facial paralysis that is neither dangerous nor contagious. It comes from the virus that causes chicken pox, which most of us had as kids. The virus often doesn't disappear, but stays in our body in a dormant state. In adulthood, it can activate as shingles or as Bell's.

The ER doctor confirmed the diagnosis. I went home and finished working with my clients. That night, one of my sons,

Benny, walked in, took one look at me and said, "Hi, Harvey Dent!" referring to the two-faced Batman villain. For the next couple of months, I endured a lot of medical regimens. Over time, the paralysis gradually went away.

But in the meantime, what a strange experience for me! I couldn't talk well, had a patch over my eye because I couldn't close it, had to drink from a straw, and had to cancel all my video and television engagements.

But I accepted the Bell's at a spiritual level. I considered it a sign from God about something, but at first I had no idea what. I told him, "I'm listening. I won't be like Pharaoh. You don't have to give me plague number two. I don't want bloody water, frogs, or flies. Please, tell me what I need to hear, and I'll respond."

In other words, *I will face the success pain that is required to eliminate the symptom pain.* Something had to be driving all this bizarre activity. I wanted to find it and fix it, despite the pain.

I have a life team consisting of several close friends, and I talked to them for a long time about the problem. Finally, one of them, Elaine Morris, who directs my leadership program in Dallas, said, "You work too much. You need a board of advisors to keep you balanced." She thought the Bell's resulted from overwork.

I hated that idea. I love my freedom, my autonomy, and my work. As I've said, I am what I consider a "happy workaholic," working not out of isolation or depression but from a love of what I'm doing and a high threshold of pain. Because of that high pain threshold, I just didn't know when I was overdoing it. If a company asked me to work with it in Baltimore on a Tuesday, and a Seattle company asked me for the same thing on a Wednesday, I tended to respond, "No problem. That's what red-eye flights are for." Sleep is something you do later ... right?

I had to admit, however, that my wife and others had already told me I'd been working too much. So I asked four close friends, all mature and accomplished, to be on my board. They all agreed, and we began meeting.

That was a game changer for me. I was transparent with them. I gave them all the documentation and information I had on every major area of my life: my life mission, goals, history, finances, relationships, even my medical conditions. They approached their new responsibility with gravity and began helping me structure my work/life balance so that life became healthier for me. I began better leveraging my time, carving out time for health and balance in my calendar, and saying no to good opportunities to save room for the right opportunities in line with my own mission.

It wasn't easy. I didn't like saying no to *any* opportunity to speak, consult, or coach, because I enjoy these activities so much. But we established yearly and monthly maximum days to work, vacation times, travel limitations, and strategic plans.

And things began to get better. I have become less rushed and less busy. My effectiveness has increased. I'm not finished with this process, but already it's yielding the right kind of fruit.

I see the Bell's as the symptom pain that drove me to the success pain of getting my life and work schedule under control. One of my doctors told me that overwork can be a contributing factor to the condition. I want to work and be productive for a long time. I have plans and dreams, like anyone else. And I think the Bell's has been the suffering in the body that is helping me be done with the sin of overwork and getting out of balance.

How about you? What symptom pain are you facing? A job, relationship, or behavioral issue? Don't make the mistake of thinking that the symptom pain is the problem. It isn't. Use these principles to help put your energy into uncovering and resolving the pain that will bring you success.

The Pain of the Grind

In helping people resolve entitlement and move on to success, I have noticed a type of success pain that individuals avoid like a bad movie. When they learn how to face it and embrace it, however, their quality of life increases exponentially. I call it the *pain of the grind*.

We experience the pain of the grind when we force ourselves to do the same action over and over again, expecting a payoff in the future. It is the way things feel when you apply discipline, diligence, and perseverance. It's not fun. It doesn't create passion. It can feel boring and dreary, as if you're grinding away on some treadmill, and you can't help wondering when it will ever stop.

And it can make you a success.

Consider a few examples of the pain of the grind:

- It's 3 p.m. at the office. You've made twenty cold calls in your sales job. You have heard rejection after rejection, and yet you have ten more sales calls to go to make quota. You feel tired and rejected (because you *have* been rejected). But you pick up the phone the twenty-first time.

- You had to set some boundaries with your teenager about her poor grades. If she doesn't make the grade threshold you set, she will lose many of her phone and social privileges. You've already been through one report card period in which she missed the mark and expressed great unhappiness, and now the new report card is no better. You have to stick with the boundary for another report card period, while she escalates, blames, whines, and tries to manipulate you. You feel battle-weary and exhausted. But you stick with it, because to give in will increase the chances that she won't succeed in school.

246

- You need more capital to fund your start-up company. The blue-sky phase was exciting and energizing. You loved the dreaming, the visioning, the plotting. Now you have to go, hat in hand, to banks, investors, and even friends, with a proposal and a well-crafted pitch. You gear up your energy for each new conversation, and it feels exhausting. But you ask for that next meeting to get calendared.

- You're on an assembly line that involves you repeating the same actions on a machine hundreds of times a day. It doesn't require a great deal of creativity, and there is little room for you to change things. It has more to do with staying precise and on target. You get bored. But you continue it, because you think about how much you love your family and how this job provides security for them.

- You are on a diet. It's the second month, and the thirty-day honeymoon is over. Your weight loss has become less dramatic, because the water weight is gone. You need your familiar comfort food to help you relax after a hard day. But you grab a raw vegetable instead. It doesn't taste nearly as good and doesn't really satisfy, although it eases the hunger. But you continue into month two; you move forward.

The pain of the grind isn't rocket science, or magic, or a miracle. It's about engaging with success pain *over time.* Not getting discouraged, distracted, or bored after the short burst of energy. It's sticking with the right things over the course of days, weeks, months, and years. The pain of the grind works on the principle that most of the significant things we need in life come from an oven, not a microwave.

Our entitlement culture resists the pain of the grind. The cop movie ends with a great gun battle in which a few minutes of strategic fighting win the day. The tabloids promise thirty pounds of weight loss in thirty days. But that's just not reality.

I have seen the pain of the grind operate in companies over and over again. The brilliant, creative, flaky executive has great ideas but just can't stick to the basics, such as finishing things, getting the reports in, checking her work, and doing the due diligence. Everyone likes her and appreciates her, but over time the company gets tired of all the collateral damage she causes. And the not-quite-as-brilliant or creative but steady and dependable person generally gets the promotions and moves on.

Commit to the oven instead of the microwave. I admit, it's not as fun. But people who continue to start over and over again, in some *Groundhog Day* fashion, have less and less fun over time. Do this right, and the reward you'll have is the fun of a great life.

Skills to Help You Do Pain Right

Unfortunately, the skill of having a functioning relationship with pain doesn't develop overnight. And most people who have a hard time sticking to something hard came from backgrounds in which no one required them to be diligent, or they had chaos in their homes, or they got by on talent and charm.

If you and pain have not been getting you to where you need to go, here are some ideas that will help you.

Ask "why" before "how." When you encounter an obstacle or a problem, don't ask, "How do I get a better lemon?" You'll save time by asking, "Why is the lemon so scrawny?" In other words, step back and train your brain to look deeper than a quick solution that probably won't work. Be patient. Insist on something more effective and revolutionary than a Band-Aid solution.

Look at patterns in your life. Are there places where you find a pattern of failure? For some people, it's when others fail to encourage them, or actually discourage them. For others, it's when life's demands take too much of their time. For others, it may be when there are no shortcuts, no quick answers. Figure out which patterns are holding you back and direct your energies toward resolving the patterns.

Be clear on the worthiness of the goal. Let yourself feel how much you want the job, the relationship, or the healthy body. Paul was clear about one of his main goals, to fulfill God's purpose for him: "I press on toward the goal to win the prize for which God has called me heavenward in Christ Jesus" (Philippians 3:14). If you "sort of" want something, I promise you that life will be hard enough and distracting enough to keep you from it.

Break it down into incremental parts. Having a smaller subgoal of a certain number of phone calls, sit-ups, or deals done in a set period of time makes it less overwhelming and manageable. You may need to have yearly, monthly, weekly, daily, or hourly subgoals. But these incremental moves add up over time. Your model of success is the ant, a genius at the pain of the grind:

> Go to the ant, you sluggard;
>> consider its ways and be wise!
> It has no commander,
>> no overseer or ruler,
> yet it stores its provisions in summer
>> and gathers its food at harvest. (Proverbs 6:6–8)

Incremental also means "take breaks." A great deal of research about the brain recommends a few minutes of break every hour to refresh your mind. That break can be a walk, a book, or a conversation.

Get engaged. The most excruciating time of any success pain is when you anticipate it. It's not when you're doing it, but when you *think* about doing it. The mind plays tricks on you:

- He's going to blow up at me if I say this.

- I will fail in this project.

- No one will want what I'm selling.

- I'm so tired that working out will be torture.

If you can just get over that hump and actually engage, things become much better. As a writer who also consults and coaches, I always feel the draw of being around people and feeling the energy from the interaction, rather than making myself get into the solitude of the writing cave for a few hours or days. I find myself making excuses to get away from the cave, thinking, *It will be boring and isolated.* But when I get into it, I find that my thoughts beget other thoughts and the creative juices start flowing. It's as if I have a stimulating conversation with myself. The engagement is everything.

Get support. Having a couple of people check in on your increments will make things much less dull and dreary. You still have a few good friends on the outside. They aren't slaving away at what you are doing. So, since they don't feel the exhaustion of your experience, they can bring in fresh perspective and energy. When I write a book, I have friends who review the day's writing with me and make comments or suggestions. Or maybe they simply enjoy talking about it with me: "in your company be refreshed" (Romans 15:32).

When you fall off the horse, get back on. If your life has not made pain your friend, you'll avoid it and try to work around it. Don't get discouraged or perfectionistic. Give yourself some grace and take the long view. Failure is learning.

For those with ADD. If you have been diagnosed with ADD, you have an extra challenge in sticking to the pain of the grind. Your condition lends itself to distractibility from repetitive tasks. I have seen this damage both careers and marriages. Just go get help.

A great deal of well-researched treatment offers effective help of all kinds. You have no reason to feel embarrassed, to feel negative about yourself, or to pretend you can just buckle down and do this. You can't. The treatments will help you follow through on the pain of the grind.

Let Pain Work for You

You don't have to enjoy pain. But use it. Deal with it competently. It will work for you.

A successful business client of mine has an approach that I have long respected; I have seen its benefits demonstrated over and over again. When he meets with his team, he starts with "What are the challenges?" instead of "Tell me the good news." He believes that when he and his team face the pain of the negative realities of struggles with sales, deliverables, and culture, they will learn from them, dig into them, and succeed. They do celebrate, and celebrate well. But they dedicate their first energies to facing the pains that keep them from their success. Bad news first, good news second.

Skills

1. **Meditate on 1 Peter 4:1.** This powerful passage is so helpful about pain. Think about the sins in your life, such as fear, perfectionism, distractibility, lack of confidence, self-absorption, or control. Then ask God to reveal to you what sufferings in the body would help you to be done

with these. He wants better soil for you, so that your life fruit is healthy.

2. **Evaluate what avoiding pain has cost you.** Write it down. Did your career suffer? Your marriage? Your health? In my leadership coaching program, I regularly ask the Misery Question: "What difficulty have you been avoiding, and what has the avoidance cost you?" One business owner said recently, "I postponed shutting down one of my sites, and it cost me several million dollars." That may sound extreme, but it's not unique—I have heard answers at a scale similar to his often. And the effects aren't always measured in dollars; it's about family and personal life as well. This skill will be a good wake-up call for you.

3. **Resource yourself.** For most of us, the pain we need to experience, whether it's having a tough talk, taking a risk, or doing repetitive and noncreative tasks, is something you know deep inside you should do. You have just been avoiding it. You need to break that pattern. Do it differently this week. Don't go into this week thinking positively that, now that it's been called to your attention, it will just happen. It won't. Life has many demands and distractions. Instead, whenever your normal planning time is (say, Monday morning), calendar a time for that meeting or activity, and ask your support team for an encouraging text or phone call. Make this the week you get it done.

CHAPTER 15

TAKE A MEANINGFUL RISK EVERY WEEK

CROSSED ARMS ARE A BAD SIGN.

When I am training a management team, the guy sitting in the back of the room with his arms crossed, leaning back, with no facial expression, is giving off a signal. He's wordlessly saying, *This is a waste of time. How soon can I get back to my desk and do some real work?* Not a good indicator of positive and energetic engagement!

On a recent training I conducted with the executives of a large company, Dave was the crossed-arms guy. He was a "quant jock," the guy who worked with complicated quantitative financial models—brilliant, focused, and a key player in the company's success.

But my training that day concerned company relationships and culture, not algorithms. I had come to work with the team on how to be emotionally open and vulnerable with each other, while still holding high performance expectations. Dave made it clear that he did not intend to go there. While the rest of the staff talked about their fears and failures, about trusting each other and connecting at deeper levels, Dave sat in silence with his arms crossed.

Most companies have a Dave at the top level. These Daves achieve their high level of success through hard work and good thinking, but they often have little self-awareness, especially in how others perceive them. And that's why they rarely make it to the top. They have no idea how to inspire trust and loyalty.

So in this meeting on that day I called him out, in a polite way. "Dave," I said, "the others have opened up about their lives. What's something you want to bring to the table?"

"I was second string on the baseball team," he replied, "and it devastated me." The comment brought a few laughs from the group.

"Hey, team," I answered, "now that we are into vulnerability, let's be serious and let Dave know how his reservation and skepticism affect you right now, in the moment."

A brief silence reigned. And then the truth teller on the team, a woman named Amy, said, "Actually, I like you, Dave, but I don't feel really safe with you." It got quiet again. Another person said, "I sometimes feel like you're judging me and so I play it safe with you." A third declared, "I avoid you because all you can talk about is work, and I get tired of that."

I stopped the feedback and asked Dave, "How are these comments affecting you?"

By this time, he had gotten quiet. He said, "I don't really know what to say. It bothers me that you guys think that. Actually, it's what my wife says to me, too."

As we continued the conversation, a funny thing happened. Dave uncrossed his arms. He became more verbal. From that point on, the training took a different, and better, turn for both Dave and the team.

Dave had trained himself never to be vulnerable in social settings, to play it safe, and to stick to left-brain tasks and thoughts. He was risk-averse in the relational and vulnerability realm. It took the team's pressure for him to begin chipping away at his fear.

The culprit here? As I got to know Dave in our one-on-one coaching sessions, it quickly became clear that his problem had originated with our culture of entitlement. He had always thought he should not *have* to take relational risks or put himself "out there." He felt it was beneath him. He shouldn't be expected to be a touchy-feely kind of guy. His culture of entitlement mantra was: *I have it together. I am above risks.*

But Dave's strategy didn't work, in either his professional life or his personal one. So he and I started working toward a different, and a more fruitful, Hard Way mantra: *I need to take risks to grow and accomplish what I want.*

Why Risk? Consider Several Great Reasons

I have never met a truly successful and healthy person who did not make meaningful risk-taking a normal part of his or her life.

I mentioned risk-taking in the chapters on admitting wrong (chapter 13) and on motivation (chapter 5). Risk is found throughout the literature of growth; it's a pervasive concept that's impossible to compartmentalize.

Consider just a few of the many benefits risk has for you:

- *Risk is your only hope for "better" in anything.* Without risk, your only path is "the same," whether in your career, love life, or some passion such as a hobby or ministry. Without risk, you are certain to do no better than the "same," if not worse. Do you really want such a path?

- *The process of risk brings out the best in you.* It forces you to think, plan, obsess, look at the facts, make judgments, and set priorities. You can't be lazy and risky at the same time.

- *Risk humbles you because it takes you to the limit of yourself.* When you get on the phone to pitch that next sale, you don't know what will happen and you can't control it. You could fail, and you wouldn't like that.

- *Risk is a great teacher.* There is no better way to learn how to run a business, play a sport, start a new relationship, or navigate your way to a better marriage than to try out things with no idea how they will wind up.

- *You feel more alive when you risk.* The adrenal glands start flushing; you get scared, excited, and energized.

The most important of these, by far, is the first one. Without risk, there is simply no path to anything you truly desire. You'll never do better than you are right now, without risk. And Hard Way living requires risk.

A Lifestyle of Cliff Diving

I once took my sons on a whitewater rafting trip in Nevada. For several days, we learned to ride the rapids and had time left over to see the sights. One afternoon, our guide took us to a cave that had an underground pool and some rock cliffs. The time had come to do a high jump from one of the cliffs, thirty feet above the water.

About twenty preteen kids had come on the trip, none of whom had ever taken a jump at that height. They hadn't, at their age, had a lot of experience in physical risks. When the guide challenged the kids to jump, there was a pause. Kids looked at the cliff, the water, at each other, and back to the water. Finally, one boy walked over to the edge AND jumped in with a large splash. When his head popped up with no blood gushing from it, the ice was broken. The rest of the kids climbed up, lined up, and got it done, with even a few cannonballs, jackknifes, and some bruises, but nothing requiring a doctor or a medevac. Then they told lies to each other at dinner that night about the trick dives they'd done.

The kids would have had a crummy time had they not jumped. If they had looked at the cliff, then the water, then walked back to our rafts—how sad and disappointing!

My point is this: *Cliff diving is a life habit, not an event.* It is a normal and necessary skill that separates winners from those who stay stuck. Winners don't get the great job and then stop. They want a great job, a great marriage, great kids, and a great life of service. They want it all, even if it involves risk and failure. They just think and behave that way in every arena of life. After they make their cliff dive and learn whatever there is to learn there, they start plotting their next risk. It never ends.

It's a good way to take on life.

Why do we love reading about Peter, the impulsive disciple? He made so many mistakes, but we admire his capacity to be a cliff diver. When he saw Jesus walking on the water, he immediately took a risk, against the laws of physics, for the sake of getting close to Jesus:

> "Lord, if it's you," Peter replied, "tell me to come to you on the water."
>
> "Come," he said.

> Then Peter got down out of the boat, walked on the water and came toward Jesus. (Matthew 14:28–29)

Peter inspires us to get out of our comfort zones. I have never met a successful person, in business or family, who did not regularly get out of their own comfort zones in this way.

What Is Your Next Cliff?

There are literally as many cliff jumps we need to take as there are areas of life. It just depends on which one you face at any given time. And you have no guarantee that things will succeed — that's why they call it a risk.

But your risks should be *meaningful*. They must make a difference to what matters to you. Skydiving and car races are risks, and they adrenalize us, but they are more about fun, excitement, and entertainment. I'm not talking about them. Meaningful risks have to do with the life you want to carve out for yourself. For example:

- Ask for a raise and risk a no.

- Work nights and weekends to start your own business and risk hours of sweat and effort if it doesn't work out.

- Let your spouse know you have a bad habit that is tearing you apart and risk a terrible reaction.

- Approach that person you find attractive and risk rejection.

- Tell your friends you can't hang out so much because you want to go to night school and risk them thinking you aren't really part of them.

- Tell your sports friends you like art, and your art friends you like sports, and risk getting ribbed by both groups.

- Have that confrontation with your young-adult child about his lack of motivation to move out of your home and assume responsibility for himself.

- Try out for a part in the community theatre and risk not getting the part.

- Have that tough talk with your spouse about how unhappy you are in the marriage and how much you want things to be better.

- Tell your boss you want to be considered for another position and risk losing the one you have.

- Start a blog and risk negative reviews.

Is your cliff in this list, or do you need to add something else here?

Traits of Great Risk Takers

In my work with executives, business owners, and successful people in general, I have found several key traits they all have in common.

They Have No Illusion of Security

Great risk takers have seen through the myth of security, for true security doesn't really exist, except within the love of God: "Those who know your name trust in you, for you, LORD, have never forsaken those who seek you" (Psalm 9:10). The rest of it can go at any time, and often does.

But I don't want to give the impression that I think all smart and ambitious people in the business world are risk takers. Many are in conflict about risk, unsure which way to go. Their thinking goes something like this: *I have a family, a mortgage, debts. I know I dream about doing something I love and running the show, but this large company has been around for a long time, has thousands of employees, and I'm doing well there.*

A few weeks later, the company undergoes a rightsizing, and those non-risk takers who wanted to stick with the company for security now get a couple of months of severance, and then what?

I work with lots of large corporations, and the CEOs and board members of any of them will tell you that there is no such thing as true security in the working world. You can be working for a Fortune 500 company. You can be working for the government. Or you can open a lemonade stand on the street corner. But don't kid yourself. In the long run, *your only guarantee of job security is that it doesn't exist.*

A client of mine in the media world was in the beginning stages of entrepreneurship. He had a dream of doing his own thing, but he had kids and obligations. He was highly regarded in his position in a large company and was clearly on his way up the ladder.

But the dream wouldn't go away. He liked his job but felt an itch that couldn't be scratched. He had ideas that simply could not be expressed in his current job. As a matter of fact, a part of him was a bit unemployable as well. He kept pushing against the conventions — not to be a pain, but because he was an autonomy freak. It was all about freedom for him.

He and his wife began to plan the dream. The first question that came up was, of course, security, since they had young kids. And they had one big obstacle to deal with: Her dad had been laid off years before, and the change had been hard on her family. They had to move often, and she couldn't go to the college she had dreamed of. She didn't want her family to experience that sort of shock and loss.

But as they thought about the dream, they identified one significant difference between her childhood and now: Her father had little control over his environment. Large-scale, tectonic market shifts had just taken place, and her father had been given no choice — he had simply been handed his pink slip.

Now, she and her husband were actually making choices to risk. *And when you make a choice to risk, you have more control. When you make a choice to stay put with the illusion of safety, you have less control.* While taking *any* risk means you can't control the outcome (or else it wouldn't be a risk), you are in more control when you have thought it through in a calculated, evaluative manner. It's far better to do your homework and invest in a start-up business, with already-discussed costs of failure built into your life and budget, than to keep pushing along on a path that will not be sustainable for you.

That realization gave my client and his wife the push they needed. They made plans, she supported him, and within a few months he had set up his new company, left the old one, and dived off the cliff. I predicted it would take three years before he could get to the same level of revenue he'd reached with the previous company.

It ended up being less than twelve months.

He attributes a great deal of his focus and success to his realization of the truth that there was in fact no trampoline under him, even in the corporate world.

When you see the reality that there truly is no security but the love of God, you are free from fear and from risk-averse behavior.

They Are Prepared to Tolerate Failure for Possible Reward

Successful people are okay if the risk fails. They don't have a "failure is not an option" stance. They have worked through what it will cost them in time, money, resources, and energy. And it may not be pleasant, but they know they will survive and that it was worth trying for it.

It takes sober thinking to thoroughly look at the downside. It is not enjoyable to think, *I may lose a lot of time, money, and energy here.* But people who don't do this can get caught up in what psychologists call catastrophic anxiety, a type of wordless panic that can freeze you up from making good decisions and being creative. As vacationers in Las Vegas say, "Don't gamble with money you can't lose." If you can live with reaping failure from the risk you sow, you are well on your way.

They Just Do Stuff

Risk takers don't wait for permission, don't wait for encouragement or prodding from others, and don't wait for a crisis. They feel the dream, they allow themselves to feel the desire, and *they act.*

They take initiative. No external person, force, or circumstance triggers them. They just do stuff. They are active, sometimes restless, looking for opportunities and ways to a better life.

The things they do might not make sense at first. They may take a course or hole up for a week thinking and brainstorming, or have lots of Starbucks conversations about the next step. But they are in motion. Doing stuff that doesn't seem all that productive is an improvement over not doing anything except the same thing you've always done.

They Normalize Risk

They see risk as something people do, not something *other* people do, and not something you do once a year when you have a big deal or crisis ahead of you. It is a human habit. The title of this chapter is intended literally: "Take a meaningful risk every week." *Every week.* From disagreeing with that controlling person in your life to being vulnerable to a friend about your failures to starting a new enterprise, do things that move you toward your desire, with no guarantee of the outcome. A week is large enough to not overwhelm you, small enough that you don't lose traction.

They Are Calculated, Not Impulsive

The truly great risk takers I have worked with are not wild-eyed adrenaline junkies. They are careful and deliberate, respect the obstacles to their risk, and take calculated risks. In the stock market, they do their research. In their marriages, they know when to push an issue and when to back off. They make their decisions after doing due diligence, and they respect the possible downside.

Keep that last point in mind. Some people are naturally fearless, and I don't mean that in a healthy way. They don't feel fear when they need to. They make awful investments, choose toxic relationships, and don't follow through on their self-care.

Others have been so controlled and careful all their lives that they sometimes reach a tipping point and behave just as the unwise risk takers do. They have gotten so tired of being afraid that they become impulsive.

So don't attempt any significant new behavior, and don't make any significant new commitment of time, money, love, or energy without prayer, thinking through the consequences, and seeking the counsel of good people.

They Create a Community of Cliff Divers

Good risk takers feel attracted to one another. They understand the stakes, support each other, challenge each other, and help one another when the chips are down. It's hard to fight against the gravitational pull of the status quo in life. Without a community of like-minded cliff divers to support them, they run out of gas and question whether they are on the right track. When they feel discouraged, they know they need others to help them keep up the pace: "And let us consider how we may spur one another on toward love and good deeds" (Hebrews 10:24).

I know a young, successful executive in his twenties who was struggling with his own desire as to whether he should transition into the film world, which he loved. Film is notoriously risky. It's a feast or famine business, and he had created a productive line of work for himself that he would have to leave behind.

He had lunch with an older friend, in his forties, who had been in both worlds. "How do I figure out the next twenty years?" he asked the older man.

"Don't," came the reply. "There are way too many variables, and you'll drive yourself crazy. Plan for the next five, do things you love, don't make dumb mistakes, and meet a whole lot of people."

The "five years instead of twenty" idea was transformative for the young man. He immediately felt a lightness inside, and creative energy began to animate his ideas and passions. Having an older and successful friend push him away from overplanning liberated him. He's still in the process of determining his next steps. But knowing his character, his talent, and his determination, I have every confidence that he will make the next big risk with a great outcome.

Get Past the Obstacles

Risk is risky. It may feel energizing, but risk has real downsides; that's why we all have messages in our heads that keep us in the illusion of security. Consider the main blocks to successful cliff-diving and how to move past them.

A Dysfunctional Fear of Failure

Normal people feel some fear of failure. That's what keeps them from throwing their lives into a black hole. Normal fear of failure makes you think again before you impulsively quit your job one day just because you had a really difficult week. You should listen to that fear.

But when you find yourself stuck in a seemingly endless cycle of rethinking, recalculating, reviewing, and polishing your idea, you may be stuck in a dysfunctional fear of failure. That fear keeps you from functioning as you need to and retards growth and progress.

A friend of mine, a gifted speaker and presenter, went out on his own. He struggled. And the bills kept coming in. He hired a business coach who looked at how he spent his time. It turned out my friend was spending 80 percent of his work time polishing his talks and PowerPoint presentations and only 20 percent of his time calling, networking, and getting speaking gigs.

When this was pointed out to him, he realized that he feared the rejection of the market. He had a critical judge in his head who personalized normal failure as "It's not just that you failed—you *are* a failure." So to avoid that condemning voice, he spent his time on safe activities that didn't put him in risk's way.

If you struggle with a dysfunctional fear of failure, do what my friend did to cure this. First, he became aware of the judge in his head. Just that awareness helped significantly. Then, when he would feel anxiety about meeting people and asking for gigs, he would call a few supportive and safe friends in what I call the "five-minute injection call." The friend would understand the fear and would counter the voice of the judge by giving him another voice: "I get it—you're scared, and you may fail. But whether you win or lose, I'm your friend and I want you to call me after you make the ask." That solved it for him. It should do the same for you.

A Tendency to Shy Away from Disappointment

If you've been disappointed too many times in the past, why risk getting let down again? This keeps many people from becoming cliff divers. The feeling hurts, so many people don't let themselves feel their passions. That way, they don't have to face the inevitable (they think) disappointment.

Disappointment problems often stem from a dependency on a certain desired outcome, and the sense that *this must happen in the right way, or it will be devastating.* Maybe the one person you'll ever love (in your mind, at least) breaks up with you. Or the tenth job interview goes south—the big one. Why put myself in a position to risk more pain and despair?

The best fix for this is to give yourself permission to have multiple answers and multiple options. People get their hearts broken all the time, and many times, after they recover, they find the great love of their lives. The fifteenth or the twenty-fifth interview works because the job-seeker didn't have that desperate, "must have" feeling. Letting go of dependency on particular and specific outcomes will free you up.

A Misplaced Faith in Rescue Wishes

Some people avoid risks because they believe that someone, somewhere, will see their plight, be sensitive to their need, and rescue them. That person will provide the money, the job, or the marriage. This is a rescue wish. It is a type of early childhood daydream that can come either from neglectful parenting or helicopter parenting, two sides of the same coin.

Rescue wishes are powerful. People who suffer from them tend to shut down and isolate in times of challenge, during the very times they should be calling up energy and activity. But their faith in the rescue wish tells them to wait and be passive—help is on the way.

The answer to the rescue wish is to abandon the desire for someone to take over and fix things and adopt instead the desire for someone to walk alongside you. It's the difference between rescue and help, between winning the lottery and getting a mentor who will show you how to learn a marketable skill. Ask for help in the form of support, acceptance, advice, ideas, and networks. But don't ask for rescue. It won't take you anywhere you need to go.

Risk a Red Back

If your choice in life is between staying on the ledge and feeling safe (and mostly dead) or becoming a cliff diver who risks a lobster-red back (but who feels fully alive), then choose risk. You'll find there is no comparison.

Make risk a weekly part of your life.

Skills

1. **Make the connection between desire and risk.** Identify what really matters to you that you don't yet have. Now—identify what risk is keeping you away from it. Make the connection between the two. The more you mentally put them together, the more you talk about them, the more you journal and pray over them, the more likely a great thing is to happen. I have seen it hundreds of times: *The desire increases and the fear of the risk decreases*. The two have an inverse relationship. Keep letting yourself feel the desire. It will help.

2. **Get the good from your life team.** A life team is a few people of good character who want you to risk and win and who will help you with that. Tell them you're afraid that if you don't get the listing for the house, you'll end up on the street with a tin cup. Have them remind you of your history, your character, and your support system. It's amazing how powerful it is to hear someone authentically see good things in you, *even things you already know*. The power of relational support cannot be overestimated.

3. **"Do stuff" for the next thirty days.** Develop this movement skill. Take small risks, a couple a week, for the

269

next month. These need to be things you don't normally do, to get your energy going:

- Be the first one in the team meeting to say what you think about the proposal, instead of waiting to see which way the political winds blow.

- When someone asks you this week how you are doing, actually tell them how you are doing.

- Ask someone for something that matters to you, instead of spending 90 percent of every conversation talking about them. They may be happy to give you the support, listening ear, love, or advice you seek.

- Get a fresh perspective on what you want out of life by talking to someone with whom you haven't discussed this. Mix up your social contacts a bit.

4. **Meditate on the parable of the talents in Matthew 25.** This is a scary passage about risk-averse behavior. Jesus praises risk, and he confronts risk avoidance. I have made this passage one of my life verses, and I think about it all the time. It has helped me choose risk when I wanted to hide my talent in the ground. And the principle has never let me down.

CONCLUSION: THE PATH

ACTUALLY, THERE *IS* AN EASY WAY. It is the yoke of Jesus, and it is identical to God's Hard Way. This is no play on words; it is real and true. From God's perspective, they are one and the same. In the words below, Jesus gives us this comfort and encouragement:

> Come to me, all you who are weary and burdened, and I will give you rest. Take my yoke upon you and learn from me, for I am gentle and humble in heart, and you will find rest for your souls. *For my yoke is easy and my burden is light.* (Matthew 11:28-30, italics added)

Jesus tells us that his yoke is easy. *But at the same time, he does not refrain from calling it a yoke.* A yoke is a device that connects you directly to the weight to be pulled—the work to be done—just as a workhorse is connected by yoke and harness to the plow to be pulled. Accepting the yoke of Jesus means committing to work—sometimes to hard work. But he still calls it easy, because it spares us and frees us from the yoke of the law.

If you have ever felt the need to strive to be good enough for God, to seek approval from others, or to perform—and still not felt acceptable no matter how hard you struggled—then you know something about the law. That yoke is impossible to bear,

271

and therein lies perfectionism, self-condemnation, guilt, and shame. It will break your back if you take it on.

It almost broke mine before I experienced God's grace. My early years in the Christian faith were marked by lots and lots of Bible study, meetings, and conversations that were ultimately driven by a desire to make myself good enough for God. I ended up exhausted and not feeling fruitful or abundant. Fortunately, a pastor friend taught me about abiding, or remaining, in Christ. He took me through Jesus's words in John 15:4:

> Remain in me, as I also remain in you. No branch can bear fruit by itself; it must remain in the vine. Neither can you bear fruit unless you remain in me.

The aha moment for me was when I realized that I don't have to be good enough for God. And I'm not. The cross freed me from that burden and helped me to experience the benefits of being loved over being good enough. I learned that it is the relationship of dependence and abiding in my connection with him that made all the difference. That has truly been the easy yoke in my life.

Yet I believe that even the way of the law, as hard as it is, is actually less difficult than the way of entitlement. Why should that be? Because the law at least drives us to hunger for and search after God. The way of entitlement, however, begins and ends with narcissism. *Attempting to be good enough for God yields more hope than demanding to be God.*

In my work with men and women, I often see a progression: Entitlement gives way to law, and then law gives way to grace. The self-absorbed person finally comes face-to-face with the reality that he is not God, nor is he as grandiose and bulletproof as he thought. This truth brings a lot of pain. So then he moves to another tactic: He tries to be very, very good, and do things very,

very well. He wants to show that he can earn his way out of his failings. But ultimately this tactic fails, too, as all our works do.

At that point, he is ready for God's Hard Way—the path that says we are all failures, that we all have to admit those failures and take responsibility for them. And then, having faced the intolerable, *we come face to face with grace.*

The grace of God is the only possible way to accept ourselves, to learn humility, to take responsibility, to make the necessary changes in our lives, and to become the individuals God designed you and me to be.

In the end, it's all about grace, the very grace of God.

So stand against entitlement in every form in which it manifests itself. Resolve your own tendencies toward the disease. Be a loving and firm force for helping those in its trap to find life and hope. And you will make the world a better place.

God bless you.

John Townsend
Newport Beach, California
2015

NOTES

1. Howard S. Friedman and Leslie R. Martin, *The Longevity Project* (New York: Hudson Street Press, 2011), 9.

2. Stephen Covey, *7 Habits of Highly Successful People* (New York: Simon & Schuster, 1989, 2004), 102–53.

3. Henry Cloud and John Townsend, *Safe People* (Grand Rapids: Zondervan, 1996).

4. Henry Cloud and John Townsend, *How to Have That Difficult Conversation You've Been Avoiding* (Grand Rapids: Zondervan, 2005).

5. Bill Hybels, *Holy Discontent* (Grand Rapids: Zondervan, 2007), 23.

6. David Allen, *Getting Things Done* (New York: Penguin Books, 2001). Kindle book, location 715.

7. Henry Cloud and John Townsend, *Boundaries* (Grand Rapids: Zondervan, 1992).

8. An article from millennialmarketing.com makes good points here, which also have application to all ages: millennialmarketing.com/2009/11/themillennials-the-roots-of-entitlement.

9. Patrick Lencioni, *The Five Dysfunctions of a Team: A Leadership Fable* (San Francisco: Jossey-Bass, 2002).

10. Rick Warren, personal communication, 2010.

11. Bill Hybels, *Axiom: Powerful Leadership Proverbs* (Grand Rapids: Zondervan, 2008). Kindle book, location 369.

12. Hal Hershfield, research from NYU's Stern School of Business, "Don't Stop Thinking about Tomorrow," *Psychology Today*, https://www.psychologytoday.com/blog/dont-delay/201403/dont-stop-thinking-about-tomorrow.

13. Henry Cloud, *9 Things You Simply Must Do to Succeed in Love and Life* (Nashville: Nelson, 2004), 69–94.

14. The first one was: Henry Cloud and John Townsend, *Boundaries: When to Say Yes and How to Say No to Take Control of Your Life* (Grand Rapids: Zondervan, 1992).

15. C. S. Lewis, *The Problem of Pain* (New York: Macmillan, 1961); this quotation is widely quoted on the internet: e.g., http://www.goodreads.com/quotes/1180-pain-insists-upon-being-attended-to-god-whispers-to-us.

Boundaries

When to Say Yes, How to Say No to Take Control of Your Life

Dr. Henry Cloud and Dr. John Townsend

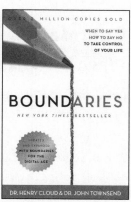

Are you in control of your life?
Do people take advantage of you?
Do you have trouble saying no?
Christians often focus so much on being loving and giving that they forget their own limits and limitations. Have you ever found yourself wondering:

- Can I set limits and still be a loving person?
- How do I answer someone who wants my time, love, energy, or money?
- Why do I feel guilty when I consider setting boundaries?

In this Gold Medallion Award–winning book, Drs. Henry Cloud and John Townsend give you biblically based answers to these and other tough questions, and show you how to set healthy boundaries with your parents, spouse, children, friends, coworkers, and even yourself.

Boundaries are personal property lines that define who you are and who you are not, and influence all areas of your life. Physical boundaries help you determine who may touch you and under what circumstances.

Mental boundaries give you the freedom to have your own thoughts and opinions.

Emotional boundaries help you deal with your own emotions and disengage from the harmful, manipulative emotions of others.

Spiritual boundaries help you distinguish God's will from your own and give you renewed awe for your Creator.

Unpacking ten "laws of boundaries," Drs. Cloud and Townsend show you how to bring new health to your relationships. You'll discover firsthand how sound boundaries give you the freedom to walk as the loving, giving, fulfilled individual God created you to be.

Available in stores and online!

Boundaries with Teens

When to Say Yes, How to Say No

*Dr. John Townsend, coauthor
of the bestselling* Boundaries

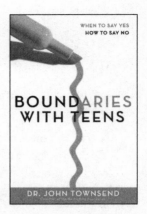

The teen years—relationships, peer pressure, school, dating, character. To help teenagers grow into healthy adults, parents and youth workers need to teach them how to take responsibility for their behavior, their values, and their lives. The coauthor of the Gold Medallion Award–winning book *Boundaries* and the father of two teenage boys brings his biblically based principles to bear on the challenging task of the teen years, showing parents:

- how to bring control to an out-of-control family life
- how to set limits and still be loving parents
- how to define legitimate boundaries for the family
- how to instill in teens a godly character

In this exciting new book, Dr. Townsend gives important keys for establishing healthy boundaries—the bedrock of good relationships, maturity, safety, and growth for teens and the adults in their lives. The book offers help in raising your teens to take responsibility for their actions, attitudes, and emotions.

Available in stores and online!

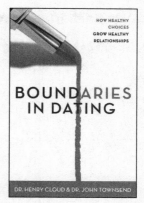

Boundaries in Marriage

Understanding the Choices That Make or Break Loving Relationships

*Dr. Henry Cloud
and Dr. John Townsend*

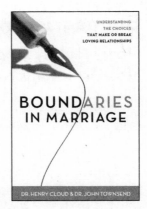

Only when you and your mate know and respect each other's needs, choices, and freedom can you give yourselves freely and lovingly to one another. *Boundaries in Marriage* gives you the tools you need. Drs. Henry Cloud and John Townsend, counselors and authors of the award-winning bestseller *Boundaries*, show you how to apply the principles of boundaries to your marriage. This long-awaited book helps you understand the friction points or serious hurts and betrayals in your marriage—and move beyond them to the mutual care, respect, affirmation, and intimacy you both long for.

Our Mothers, Ourselves

How Understanding Your Mother's Influence Can Set You on a Path to a Better Life

Dr. Henry Cloud and Dr. John Townsend

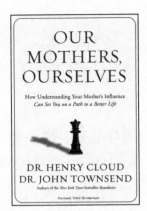

She shaped you in ways that would surprise you both.
—Craig Groeschel, senior pastor of LifeChurch.tv

No one has influenced the person you are today the way your mother has.

The way she handled your needs as a child has shaped your worldview, your relationships, your marriage, your career, your self-image—your life.

Our Mothers, Ourselves helps you identify areas that need reshaping, make positive choices for personal change, and establish a mature relationship with Mom today.

Drs. Henry Cloud and John Townsend steer you down a path of discovery and growth beyond the effects of six common mom types:

- The Phantom Mom
- The China Doll Mom
- The Controlling Mom
- The Trophy Mom
- The Still-the-Boss Mom
- The American Express Mom

You'll learn how your mom affected you as a child and may still be affecting you today. And you'll find a realistic and empowering approach to filling your unmet mothering needs in healthy, life-changing ways through other people.

Our Mothers, Ourselves is a biblical route to wholeness and growth, to deeper and more satisfying bonds with your family, friends, and spouse—and to a new, healthier way of relating to your mother today.

Available in stores and online!

Dr. John Townsend has brought his proven counseling and leadership model to Huntington University, forming the Townsend Institute for Leadership and Counseling. The first of its kind, the Townsend Institute will provide master's degree programs in counseling and organizational leadership, as well as a credential in executive coaching, counseling, or leadership. Dr. Townsend will be personally involved in teaching and he has assembled a strong faculty who are renowned experts and bestselling authors in their own fields.

TOWNSEND INSTITUTE
FOR LEADERSHIP & COUNSELING
AT HUNTINGTON UNIVERSITY